Deirdre Boyd was born and educated in Dublin, Ireland, and has lived in London since 1981. After a lengthy and successful career editing commercial magazines, she recognized and addressed her own addictions. She has since turned her talents to the benefit of charities including the Sick Children's Trust, Children In Hospital, Turning Point and the Chemical Dependency Centre, simultaneously training in psychotherapy and counselling.

In 1993 she was asked to join the Addiction Recovery Foundation where she is now manager and edits its *Addiction Counselling World* magazine, the *only* publication in the UK devoted to recovery from addiction.

The author has practised all the recovery techniques recommended in this book.

THE ELEMENT GUIDE SERIES

The Element Guide series addresses important psychological and emotional issues in a clear, authoritative and straightforward manner. The series is designed for all people who deal with these issues as everyday challenges. Each book explores the background, possible causes and symptoms where appropriate, and presents a comprehensive approach to coping with the situation. Each book also includes advice on self-help, as well as where – and when – to turn for qualified help. The books are objective and accessible, and lead the reader to a point where they can make informed decisions about where to go next.

In the same series

• THE ELEMENT GUIDE •

ADDICTIONS

Your Questions Answered

Deirdre Boyd

ELEMENT

Shaftesbury, Dorset • Boston, Massachusetts
Melbourne, Victoria

© Element Books Limited 1998
Text © Deirdre Boyd 1998

First published in Great Britain in 1998 by
Element Books Limited
Shaftesbury, Dorset SP7 8BP

Published in the USA in 1998 by
Element Books, Inc.
Boston, MA 02114

Published in Australia in 1998 by
Element Books
and distributed by Penguin Australia Limited
487 Maroondah Highway
Ringwood, Victoria 3134

Cover design by Slatter–Anderson
Phototypeset by Intype London Ltd
Printed and bound in Great Britain by
Biddles Ltd, Guildford & King's Lynn

British Library Cataloguing in Publication
data available
Library of Congress Cataloging in Publication
data available

ISBN 1–86204–180–6

Note from the Publisher

Any information given in any book in *The Element Guide* series is not intended to be taken as a replacement for medical advice. Any person with a condition requiring medical attention should consult a qualified medical practitioner or suitable therapist.

The *DSM-IV* symptoms in Chapter 2 and Appendix II have been reprinted with permission from the *Diagnostic and Statistical Manual of Mental Disorders, Fourth Edition*, American Psychiatric Association, 1994. The Twelve Steps are reproduced in Chapter 7 with the permission of Alcoholics Anonymous.

Contents

Dedication and Acknowledgments

This is both a dedication and acknowledgment to: the authors and publishers who gave permission to quote their works, particularly Wally Beirne, Jerry Moe and Gary Seidler; Sally Benjamin, Gerald Deutsch, Dr Kathy Hirsch, Dennis Hyde and Tammy Bell for their valuable information; Addiction Recovery Foundation trustees Benjamin Mancroft, Leslie Griffiths, David Macmillan, John Fenston, Tristan Millington-Drake, Peter Morris and Martin Noel-Buxton; my agent Serafina Clarke and editor Grace Cheetham; Molly Parkin and al kennedy for believing I had a book in me; Dr Jacqueline Chang for checking the book and for support; Professors Chris Cook and David Nutt for proofing the neurochemistry; my long-time colleague John Porter without whom I would not have finished the book on time; Lynda Pritchard who paid the highest compliment by putting some of the book's suggestions into practice!; Broadreach House, Tony Hazzard and Maureen McGee; Wang (UK) to whom I owe my life; Caroline A, Ron Condon, Rosa Della-Tolla, Tony and Janet, and Julius Gibbs, Dee and John Harvey, Sheila Holmes, James Kearney, Laurie Lipton, Bruce Lloyd, Edwina Mansell, Laurence McMorrow, Claudia Peres, Sheila Powney, Samira Rekab, Helen Sheridan, Mark Sherry, Daphne Thomas and Dr Michael Wilks for invaluable support; to Jane, who could not escape through addiction; Rua and Buachaillin; my multitude of cousins, Bill and uncle Liam; my enormous family, particularly *my father Harry and mother Kitty.*

Introduction

Just for today, I will allow myself to be as happy as I want to be.
'JUST FOR TODAY', ALCOHOLICS ANONYMOUS

Addiction is probably the only illness which you must understand in order to recover from it. By the time you have finished this book, you will certainly have that understanding. In fact, as the book contains the latest information from the best sources that I can lay my hands on in my professional capacity as editor of the only UK magazine devoted to recovery (*Addiction Counselling World*), you will have as much information as many professionals in the field.

Sufferers, their families and their friends usually feel powerless to stop the damage done by and to an addict, and look on helplessly. The aim of this book is to explain what is happening, to take away that feeling of powerlessness and to guide both sufferer and those close to him or her towards a life of help, support and peace of mind.

Chapter 1 identifies features which are common to all addictions. These similarities highlight the fact that you can also find similarities in solutions and sources of help.

Chapter 2 follows this with checklists of symptoms for specific kinds of addiction, both chemical (ie alcohol and drugs) and non-chemical (ie behaviours such as bingeing, working, shopping or gambling), and for obsessive-compulsive disorders.

Chapter 3 looks at the 'causes' of addiction. Ground-breaking research in the last few years shows that both substance and behavioural addictions are linked to pre-existing chemical imbalances in the body. Potential addicts have low levels of 'feelgood' chemicals which occur naturally in other people's bodies. They can only 'feel good' by using an artificial substance which triggers these chemicals – but simultaneously sets up the addictive process. Learning how this chemical chain works can help us to understand that stopping has nothing to do with intelligence or willpower – only with not taking that *first* drink, drug or other object of addiction which sets up the chemical chain.

The low levels of feelgood chemicals can be further depleted by childhood events. By looking back at these events, we can put them in context and react to them in a positive way. This raises the levels of feelgood chemicals in a natural way.

Chapter 4 details self-help tactics for emergencies when you feel you *must* use your addiction. Chapter 5 shows how to use 'boundaries' – invisible physical and emotional shields – to protect you while you are learning both these tactics and the longer-term strategies described in Chapter 6. All these tactics are worth practising when professional therapists are not available, between therapy sessions even when you have a therapist, and to see how much you can improve things by yourself.

If there is a '12-Step' group for your particular addiction, you might not need to seek professional help as it will support your self-management and suggest even more ways of recovery. Chapter 7 explains exactly what a 12-Step group is and what it can offer you.

If, despite all the above, you find that you still cannot stop your addiction, it is time to seek professional help. Chapter 8 explains the different types of treatment available: individual, group, daycare and residential. It also explains what to look for in your treatment provider, and what you might expect in the course of therapy.

Appendix I deals with the special case of adolescents.

Most teenagers will not have lived long enough to have committed often enough the highly shaming, damaging actions which older adults have gone through in the course of their addiction, and which forced them to seek help. However, we can open their eyes and minds to the value of life without addiction.

Offenders in the courts and criminal justice system are sometimes reluctant to enter treatment also. One of the adolescents' programmes will work for them, too.

Appendix II deals with the special cases of 'dual disorders': another disorder accompanying the addiction and which may have been masked by it. The most common are depression, personality disorder and schizophrenia. It is vital that these cases are diagnosed – dual disorder must mean dual recovery. This appendix also deals with an often-neglected minority: people with physical disabilities. Carers often mistakenly think that disabled people are an exception – that their addiction is all disabled people have to make a hard life easier. But the addiction is the most crippling disability of all and must be tackled.

Finally, at the end of this book, there is a list of helpful addresses, and some suggestions for further reading (this list also includes details of all the books and magazines mentioned in the text).

I would be delighted to hear from readers who have found this book helpful. You can contact me c/o the publisher or at *Addiction Counselling World*, 122A Wilton Road, London SW1V 1JZ, UK.

CHAPTER 1

About Addiction

I held a high-profile job with a multinational company. I owned my own house. I was in a seven-year relationship. I was successful. But I was miserable.

What my family didn't know was that I had started drinking in the office, endangering my job. I was two months in arrears with my mortgage. Despite my good salary, I couldn't pay the bills. My boyfriend was becoming increasingly violent and insulting. People stopped inviting me to social events.

CATHERINE

I grew up thinking that workaholism was a virtue. I turned down social engagements because I 'had to' work. I missed family events because I 'had to' work – it was the only excuse my workaholic family both understood and accepted. In the end, I couldn't have any conversation unless it was about work. I socialized only with work colleagues. In 17 years of working, I took only three weeks' holiday. By my late 30s, I was very lonely.

I regularly did three people's jobs yet did not earn as much as counterparts who held only one post. I feared that if I asked for a pay rise I might lose my job. I was like an alcoholic who was being paid to drink – there was no way I would question the payment.

JOHN

Sometimes there is just a hint or two of addiction, that something is not quite right. It becomes far more painful if you wait till later, when you are desperate to stop and don't know how to. It is equally painful to watch someone close sink into the degradation which accompanies full-blown addiction. On the way, everyone will have suffered increasing damage from rages, arguments, financial difficulties, social embarrassments, stress, unpredictability, accidents and injuries, and emotional and physical illnesses.

The good news is: there are solutions which work. And you do not have to reach the worst stages of addiction before you try them and reverse your situation.

This chapter looks at what is common to all addictions. It also gives a checklist for the 'codependency' that accompanies every addiction. Recovery from codependency is part of recovery from addiction.

THE COMMON FEATURES

First of all, a definition of what addiction is *not*. It is nothing to do with lack of willpower or intelligence. In fact, if you are an addict, you probably have above-normal rations of both willpower and intelligence.

There are many paradoxes. For example, whether you are addicted to a substance or to a behaviour, you are looking for an escape from pain of which you may no longer be aware or from memories which you may no longer consciously remember.

Addicts have low self-esteem. They can hate themselves, even though they can present a successful mask to the world (and gamblers, for example, feel a sense of over-confidence, power and control). Addicts often feel ashamed, and that they deserve to be punished. They can be lonely, perhaps especially so when surrounded by friends.

Addicts are preoccupied with their substance or behaviour. They can spend large chunks of time not only 'using' (ie using their addiction) but also thinking about using or giving up, trying to fund the addiction, getting into activities which help them to use, and trying to make up for the consequences of a bad bout of using.

Addicts are drawn to acquaintances of similar habits, so

that their own behaviour does not look too bad beside them.

If you are an addict, you have probably already noticed that you are excessively concerned with the approval of others. Despite your downward spiral, you are usually a perfectionist.

Most addicts are cut off – dissociated – from their feelings and their bodies, so much so that they don't even know it. When addicts are asked how they feel, they inevitably start their reply with 'I think . . .'. The reaction comes from the intellect, not the body. For instance, have you scared people with your rage, then denied you were angry – and meant it? When someone has commented that you looked upset, have you denied the evidence of their eyes, and believed that you told the truth?

Sadly, addicts are not cut off from every feeling. If you are reading this book, you will have felt the most intense fear, shame, loneliness, desperation and increasing despair. The only euphoric feeling has probably come from excitement, an adrenalin buzz. This is why the search for excitement can be both an addiction in itself and a spur in other addictions.

All addicts need more and more of their addiction to achieve the same level of euphoria or intoxication; you get less and less satisfaction from the same 'volume' of addiction. Almost every addict has tried to control, reduce or stop using but has managed to succeed for limited periods only, if at all, despite best intentions and efforts.

You, or someone close to you, might also have jeopardized or lost close relationships, educational opport unities and jobs. You or they might have engaged in 'bail out' behaviour, turning to family or others for help with financial or other problems – but not with the addiction itself.

You or they might have said something on the lines of 'If you had my problems, you would drink/drug/use, too'. This is called 'denial' for it is the addiction which causes the problems in the first place.

An outside observer will notice a pattern to addiction: preoccupation, denial, craving and relapse into the addiction and its accompanying behaviour, all getting progressively worse.

I believe that one vital ingredient in addiction is a grief which was not allowed to be expressed in childhood so that it intensified, ignored, over decades. This grief can be from emotional, physical or sexual abuse or the loss of a loved one through death, divorce or separation. Tracing the source and grieving in recovery is a sure sign of good progress.

CODEPENDENCY

I have never known an addict who was not also codependent. Codependency – the 'in' word of the 1980s – is the addiction to looking elsewhere. This can include substances or behaviours but is mainly taken to mean a certain type of dependence on other people.

There is a joke which might help to explain it: 'A codependent is someone who finds out how you are before they can tell you how they are'. Another descriptive joke is: 'When a codependent is about to die, someone else's life flashes before their eyes'. A codependent will have a match/lighter ready before someone even knows they want a cigarette.

In other words, if you are codependent, people's reactions matter so much to you that, if you cannot handle them, you can turn to addiction instead. How to handle your reaction to other people is learned through the 'boundaries' explained in Chapter 5.

Codependents act as though they have extrasensory perception. In other words, they guess what other people are feeling or might feel towards a particular situation, then alter all their actions around that potential reaction so as 'not to upset anyone'.

Codependents cannot express their own wants and

needs because they do not know what they are, being used to subjugating them to those of others. This can lead to mental and physical illnesses. The whole subject is explained in more detail in *Co-Dependence: Healing the Human Condition* by Dr Charles Whitfield.

You can become codependent not only on people who are close to your heart but even on people you do not like, such as a nuisance neighbour. You can become as preoccupied with that bad neighbour and their unneighbourly actions as another codependent might be with their partner.

Below are some of the 31 questions Dr Whitfield uses to diagnose codependency (*see also* the questions on codependent relationships in Chapter 6):

1 Do you seek approval and affirmation?
2 Do you fail to recognize your accomplishments?
3 Do you fear criticism?
4 Do you have a need for perfection?
5 Are you uneasy when your life is going smoothly and do you continually anticipate problems?
6 Do you care for others easily, but find it hard to care for yourself?
7 Do you attract/seek people who tend to be compulsive?
8 Do you cling to relationships?
9 Is it hard for you to relax and have fun?
10 Do you have an over-developed sense of responsibility?
11 Do you have a tendency towards chronic fatigue, aches and pains?
12 Do you have difficulty asking for what you want from others?

Codependency can leave you feeling so empty that you try to fill that emptiness in unhealthy ways which lead to emotional and physical illness. Again, the solution comes from using the 'boundaries' introduced in Chapter 5.

ADDICTIVE SOCIETY

We live in an addictive society. Everyone will feel some of the symptoms described in this and the following chapter. This does not necessarily mean that you are an addict. The question is, how much these feelings affect your life.

Recovering from addiction means a new, more fulfilling and much happier way of life. The trials of everyday life must still be dealt with, but our attitude to them changes.

CHAPTER 2

Checklists for Specific Addictions

I met Peter while on holiday abroad and we had a wonderful time. He had a great body, although I did wonder about his preoccupation with bodybuilding. He also ate and drank a lot but he said that he rarely did so at home.

When he invited me round to his place two weeks later, we bumped into a pal who greeted him with the words 'Nice to see you sober for once'.

I don't want to get into a relationship with someone who has a drink or food problem. I know it will all turn sour. But I do want him. Is he really addicted?

ROBI

I noticed Anne at lunch because she was hiding a slice of brown bread under her hand, sliding it off the table on to her lap. When she left, she was still hiding it. It was very peculiar because she could just have eaten it openly, like everyone else at the table.

A few nights later, I switched on the kitchen light and found that she had been standing in the dark, rooting in the food cupboards. It's not as though she was stealing a lot of food, and she did have a right to it, anyway. I just couldn't understand why she was taking it like a thief. She looked so guilty at being caught.

PATRICIA

How can you know if someone close to you is addicted? This chapter gives checklists of symptoms for specific addictions. Some are medical criteria, others have been compiled by specialists in their fields with decades of experience. These checklists can confirm whether you need to take action or not. If you are worried about someone you can show the checklists to them. You might not get any immediate reaction – you might even be met with anger – but you will have sown the seed of recovery. People believe what they see written in black and white far more than something they hear.

Perhaps you already know you have a problem and have decided to do something about it. In that case, I hope that the checklists will reassure you that you are not alone, that you are neither 'mad' nor 'bad' but similar to a lot of other people, and that you can recover from the illness as others with these symptoms have done.

How do we define addiction or substance dependence? For the purposes of this book, we shall use 'addiction' as the all-embracing description accepted by most of the general public. But it is worth knowing that even professionals working in the treatment field do not always agree on the terminology.

'Dependency' is used as often as 'dependence', and 'chemical' as often as 'substance'. Some professionals also define addiction as applying only to a mood-altering chemical/drug/substance and dependency as applying to behaviours to achieve the same effect, such as gambling or workaholism. Still others prefer 'dependency' to describe people who are emotionally dependent only or physically dependent only (rather than both physically and emotionally dependent) on a substance. Yet others may prefer the words 'abuse' or 'misuse'.

DRUGS

This section is concerned with 'drugs of choice': alcohol, nicotine and caffeine as well as illegal and prescribed drugs.

'Probably the best way to see alcoholism or drug addiction is as a progressive fatal disease with established genetic and brain-chemical factors, and is seen in behaviours such as loss of control over drinking/drugging, denial and craving,' states Dr Michael Wilks of the Medical Council on Alcoholism in London. The description sounds daunting, but you can send alcohol and drug addiction into lifelong remission.

The most widely acknowledged definition of substance dependence was published in 1994 by the American Psychiatric Association in its *DSM-IV* diagnostic manual. The *DSM-IV* calls it a group of mental, physical and behavioural symptoms showing 'continued use of the substance despite significant substance-related problems. There is a pattern of repeated self-administration that usually results in tolerance, withdrawal and compulsive drug-taking behaviour.'

'Tolerance' is either a need for markedly increased amounts of the substance to achieve intoxification/desired effect, or a markedly reduced effect despite continued use of the same amount. When an increased dosage no longer affects your feelings – a stage for which you can wait 10 years – you can get such a shock that you try recovery.

'Withdrawal' signs can develop within hours or days after stopping or reducing substance use. Many people are familiar with the phrase 'cold turkey' to describe heroin withdrawal without medication.

If you have tried to withdraw from alcohol, you may have suffered sweating, high pulse rate, hand tremors, insomnia, nausea or vomiting, hallucinations, anxiety or fits.

The symptoms of withdrawal from amphetamines or cocaine include dysphoria (the opposite of euphoria), fatigue, unpleasant dreams, insomnia or hypersomnia (excess sleep), increased appetite and slowed or agitated, reactions.

The symptoms of withdrawal from opioids – morphine, heroin, codeine, methadone, even diarrhoeal agents and cough suppressants – include dysphoria, nausea or vomiting, muscle aches, crying, running nose, pupillary dilation, goose pimples or sweating, diarrhoea, yawning, fever and insomnia.

Nicotine withdrawal is easy to recognize. Its symptoms are depression, insomnia, irritability, frustration or anger, anxiety, difficulty concentrating, restlessness, decreased heart rate and increased appetite.

Caffeine withdrawal symptoms include fatigue or drowsiness, anxiety or depression and nausea or vomiting.

The symptoms of substance dependence

Below are the *DSM-IV* criteria for substance dependence.

1 Tolerance (increased amounts/reduced effects).
2 Withdrawal syndrome, or using another substance to avoid withdrawal symptoms.
3 Often using larger amounts or using for longer periods than intended.
4 A persistent desire or unsuccessful efforts to cut down or control substance use.
5 Spending much time obtaining the substance – for example, visiting multiple doctors or off-licences, driving long distances.
6 Giving up or reducing important social, occupational or recreational activities because of substance use.
7 Continuing substance use despite knowing you have a persistent or recurrent physical or psychological problem likely to have been caused or exacerbated by the substance – for example, using cocaine despite getting cocaine-induced depression or drinking despite knowing that it is making your ulcer worse.

If items 1 and 2 are not present, there is no physical dependence (yet).

The symptoms of substance abuse

Some people can abuse substances without being dependent on them – they can stop. But during a 12-month period they will show, like addicts, one or both of the following signs of clinically significant distress.

1 Recurrent substance use resulting in a failure to fulfil major obligations at work, school or home – for example, absenteeism, poor work performance, suspensions or expulsions from school, neglect of children or household.
2 Substance is used in physically hazardous situations – for example, when driving or operating a machine.

The important point is that, while abusing your drug of choice, you can suffer the same medical and social damage as addicts.

If you have recognized your own behaviour in any of the symptoms in the preceding sections, you have taken the vital first step into recovery. With recognition comes the beginning of the end of your addiction.

FOOD

Almost every one of the women I know who have exceptionally good figures suffer from a food disorder and continuously think themselves too fat. In my experience, people who are 'very average' or 'mildly plump' are happier with their imperfect figures than food addicts are with their near-perfect ones.

Sadly, with the growing pressure by society for super-thin super-model figures, studies have discovered a significant number of children as young as six to be worried about their body image.

Food addictions are generally divided into two types: anorexia nervosa and bulimia nervosa. There are also overeaters, who see themselves as smaller than they are, whereas anorexics and bulimics see themselves at least 30 per cent larger than they actually are.

Anorexics usually starve themselves, although a few also binge and purge like bulimics. Adults with anorexia have been admitted to hospital weighing as little as 4 stone (25 kilos) – seeing themselves as overweight all the way there. But the most life-threatening eating disorder is suffered by people who swing between anorexia and bulimia, because the strain on the body from the effects of starving then bingeing and purging is so great.

If you are anorexic, you might have tried to hide your behaviour by saying that you are becoming vegan or obsessively searching out healthfood shops. You may have exercised addictively to lose weight or, in the States particularly, become addicted to 'cut and tuck' – plastic surgery, liposuction and so on.

The symptoms of anorexia nervosa

Again, the most widely used definition of anorexia is to be found in the *DSM-IV* manual published by the American Psychiatric Association in 1994.

1 Refusal to maintain body weight at/above a minimal normal weight for age and height. (Body weight is usually less than 85 per cent of what it should be.)
2 Intense fear of gaining weight or becoming fat, even though underweight.
3 Disturbance in body image. (Sufferer sees all or a specific part of the body as fat, even though underweight.)
4 In women, absence of at least three consecutive menstrual cycles.

Julia Buckroyd, in another book in this series, *Anorexia and Bulimia*, lists the following characteristics of anorexia:

- hair loss
- insomnia
- low body temperature and heart rate
- feeling cold/poor circulation
- lanugo growth – fine hair growing all over the body, including the face

- dry skin and brittle nails
- low blood pressure

Semistarvation as an anorexic can affect most of your body organs, as can the use of laxatives, diuretics and enemas. Anaemia is a common side-effect.

The symptoms of bulimia nervosa

If you are a bulimic, you indulge in binge eating and compensatory purging to prevent weight gain. You also try to eat in secrecy – see Anne's story on the first page of this chapter.

You might plan an eating binge in advance and not stop until you are painfully full. You might then hate yourself for your lack of control. This is worse than anorexia in that you can feel that you are a 'failed anorexic'.

The following definition of bulimia nervosa again comes from the *DSM-IV*.

1 Recurrent binge eating – ie eating in one period of time (for example, in any two-hour period) more food than most people would eat in a similar time in similar circumstances – accompanied by a sense of lack of control over the eating.
2 Recurrent inappropriate compensatory behaviour to prevent weight gain, such as: vomiting; misuse of laxatives, diuretics, enemas or other medications; fasting; or excessive exercise.
3 Both the above occur, on average, at least twice a week for three months.
4 Self-evaluation is unduly influenced by body shape and weight.

In addition, you can damage your tooth enamel as a result of persistent vomiting, and get bad breath, digestive disorders and irritation of your throat and mouth.

Just as there are people who abuse mood-altering substances but are not addicted, there are people who 'comfort
eat' or compulsively overeat. This is nevertheless a
behaviour pattern that causes great distress. Unlike bulimics, comfort eaters do not usually compensate by
overexercising, vomiting or taking laxatives. They are,
therefore, more noticeable by their large size.

Finally, chocolate. There have been claims that chocolate,
or cocoa, releases chemicals in the brain which produce
effects similar to those of marijuana. But the latest scientific
opinion is that there is little in cocoa to make it addictive
and that 'chocoholics' are, in fact, affected by the food's
sugar and fatty texture.

GAMBLING AND EXCITEMENT

Addictive gambling is persistent and disrupts personal,
family or vocational pursuits. Most gamblers say that they
are seeking 'action' – euphoria or an adrenalin buzz – more
than money.

Gambling mirrors chemical addiction in that increasingly
large bets or greater risks might be needed to produce the
desired level of excitement. Like chemical addiction, there
was probably euphoria at the beginning, triggered by a big
win either by the gambler or someone they were with. You
might also continue your addiction despite repeated efforts
to control, reduce or stop your behaviour.

When you have exhausted your financial resources on
your addiction, you are even more likely to turn to forgery,
fraud, theft or embezzlement than chemical addicts,
especially if you find yourself chasing your losses, often
with bigger bets or bigger risks. All gamblers chase for
short periods, but the long-term chase is characteristic of
gambling addiction.

Gamblers differ from other addicts in that they feel a
false overconfidence or sense of power and control. They
might be superstitious. They probably also differ from

other addicts in that they recognize their gambling as the cause of their problems.

Gambling usually begins in early adolescence for men and later in life for women.

The symptoms of addictive gambling

You must show five or more of the following, according to the *DSM-IV*:

1 Preoccupation with gambling
2 Need to gamble with increasing amounts of money in order to achieve the desired excitement
3 Repeated unsuccessful efforts to control, cut back or stop gambling
4 Restlessness or irritability when attempting to cut down or stop gambling
5 Gambling to escape problems or relieve dysphoria
6 After losing money gambling, often returning another day to get even ('chasing' your losses)
7 Lying to family members, therapists or others to conceal the extent of involvement with gambling
8 Having committed illegal acts such as forgery, fraud, theft or embezzlement to finance gambling
9 Having jeopardized or lost a significant relationship, job or educational or career opportunity because of gambling
10 Relying on others to provide money to relieve a desperate financial situation caused by gambling
11 Gambling behaviour not accounted for by a 'manic episode'.

As with substance-based addictions, recovery from addictive gambling is possible through sharing with people in similar positions, experiencing withdrawal symptoms with the support of family and friends, learning how to problem-solve and enjoying the benefits of more positive thinking.

WORK

Workaholism is known as the 'respectable addiction' but it has many of the devastating consequences of other addictions. When I first addressed my own addictions, I was asked 'Are you a kind person? Are you a nasty person? Are you fun loving?' I could not answer a single question. I knew how I wrote and I knew how I produced magazines. My whole identity lay in my job. I had no sense of self outside work.

In Japan, overwork is so common that 10,000 workers a year drop dead from putting in 60- to 70-hour working weeks. The Japanese have coined the term *karoshi*, which means death from overwork.

According to Workaholics Anonymous, if you answer 'yes' to three or more of the following questions there is a chance that you are a workaholic or well on your way to becoming one.

1 Do you get more excited about your work than about family or anything else?
2 Are there times when you can charge through your work and other times when you can't get anything done?
3 Do you take work with you to bed? on weekends? on holiday?
4 Is work the activity you like to do best and talk about most?
5 Do you work more than 40 hours a week?
6 Do you turn your hobbies into money-making ventures?
7 Do you take complete responsibility for the outcome of your work efforts?
8 Have your family or friends given up expecting you on time?
9 Do you take on extra work because you are concerned that it won't otherwise get done?

10 Do you underestimate how long a project will take and then rush to complete it?

11 Do you believe that it is all right to work long hours if you love what you are doing?

12 Do you get impatient with people who have other priorities than work?

13 Are you afraid that if you don't work hard, you will lose your job or be a failure?

14 Is the future a constant worry for you even when things are going very well?

15 Do you do things energetically and competitively including play?

16 Do you get irritated when people ask you to stop doing your work in order to do something else?

17 Have your long hours hurt your family or other relationships?

18 Do you think about your work while driving, falling asleep or when others are talking?

19 Do you work or read during meals?

20 Do you believe that more money will solve the other problems in your life?

You will be glad to know that abstinence from work is not the solution for recovery! Instead, it is a matter of learning how to balance work with the rest of your life. There are tips specifically for recovery from workaholism in Chapter 6.

SHOPPING

Compulsive spenders get a buzz from the process of spending, not from what is being bought. They have no respect for money, but insist that to have none would incur immense withdrawal symptoms, just as any alcoholic or drug addict would experience.

Compulsive spenders are also thrilled at the thought of *not* getting caught by friends, family or loved ones. Often the theft of money, credit cards or cheque books creates feelings similar to those experienced while shopping.

Shopaholics feel an intense sense of their own value and high self-esteem while spending, and the complete opposite of this when not.

Ken Dyer, managing director of the Patsy Hardy Centre which treats shopaholics as well as other addicts, offers the following list of questions to determine whether you are a compulsive spender.

1 Do you feel an inner warmth and strong sense of well-being while you are out shopping?
2 Do you really need what you are purchasing?
3 Can you afford to buy what you are buying?
4 Do you have purchases at home that are duplicated?
5 Do you have purchases at home that you have not opened?
6 Do you owe money because of your spending?
7 Have you stolen in order to spend?
8 Has your spending caused marital or family problems?
9 Have you ever been in trouble with the police as a result of your spending?
10 Are you regularly taking any alcohol or medication?
11 Do you eat three regular meals each day?
12 Do you find that your behaviour towards others changes when you have no money or cannot get out to the shops?
13 Can you stop spending without suffering any major crisis?

The Patsy Hardy Centre also lists effects such as lying/cheating/stealing, large debts, loss of sleep, night sweats, loss of appetite, use of other mood-altering chemicals and behaviours, mood swings, imprisonment and even death.

Compulsive spenders can be treated in a similar way to other addicts.

LOVE, SEX, RELATIONSHIPS

Love and sex have been described as the most powerful drugs in the world. They can, indeed, be encouraged by society – but have the same effects and consequences as all the other addictions described in this chapter.

You can be blind to the world, going through the pattern of craving, tolerance, withdrawal and relapse. Tolerance here means that you can use more and more of your addiction – perhaps more frequent sex with more partners or more violent or pornographic sex – to feel something like your initial arousal. I know one sex addict who had over a hundred partners in a year yet could no longer reach orgasm. Another put up with a violent partner 'because the sex was great'.

Withdrawal can lead to anxiety, loneliness, grief and a feeling of 'I can never live without him/her'. You then chase your ex-partner or search immediately for another one to fill the gap. And, of course, if you are making such a quick decision it is unlikely to be the right decision.

In love addiction particularly, there is a feeling of 'It's us against the world'. The outside world is gradually cut off, as is dealing with day-to-day reality. Love and sex are such powerful drugs that people held in their grip become just as blind to what's going on around them as people who are addicted to alcohol, cocaine or heroin.

It can sometimes be hard to tell love and sex addiction apart, particularly in a society which couples them together. But love addiction can involve a preoccupation with romantic dreams and fantasies – soft lights, music, knights in shining armour – whereas preoccupation with sex usually involves specific planning about the sex act itself. Of course, you can be both sex and love addicted.

The following questions to assess whether you have a problem with sex or love addiction come from Sex Addicts Anonymous (SAA).

1 Do you keep secrets about your sexual or romantic

activities from those important to you? Do you lead a double life?

2 Have your needs driven you to have sex in places or situations or with people you would not normally choose?

3 Do you find yourself looking for sexually arousing articles or scenes in newspapers, magazines or other media?

4 Do you find that romantic or sexual fantasies interfere with your relationships or prevent you facing problems?

5 Do you often want to get away from a sex partner after having sex? Do you often feel remorse, shame or guilt after a sexual encounter?

6 Do you feel shame about your body or your sexuality, so that you avoid touching your body or engaging in sexual relationships? Do you fear that you have no sexual feelings, that you are asexual?

7 Does each new relationship continue to have the same destructive patterns which prompted you to leave the last relationship?

8 Is it taking more variety and frequency of sexual and romantic activities than previously to bring the same levels of excitement and relief?

9 Have you ever been arrested or are you in danger of being arrested because of your voyeurism, exhibitionism, prostitution, sex with minors, indecent phone calls etc?

10 Does your pursuit of sex or romantic relationships interfere with your spiritual beliefs or development?

11 Do your sexual activities include the risk, threat or reality of disease, pregnancy, coercion or violence?

12 Has your sexual or romantic behaviour ever left you feeling hopeless, alienated from others or suicidal?

If you answered 'yes' to more than one of these questions, SAA recommends that you seek additional literature or attend one of its meetings. Abstinence is usually recommended for a year – not for life! – while you learn how to stand back and make healthy, objective choices.

RELIGION

I remembered waking up one morning when I was eight years old to find a Catholic priest in my bed. I remembered him cuddling me and touching me at night. But my family behaved as though nothing had happened. My mother was so besotted with religion that she was blind to any imperfections in a priest. She believed his story that he had made his way to the guest bedroom after dinner.

MARIA

Some people can be so preoccupied with religion and its rites that, as with other addictions, they are unaware of events going on around them. They will hear no talk which threatens their addiction.

As with work, religious addiction can be difficult to pinpoint because devotion to religion is worthy – so using it as a cover for compulsive behaviours is very effective. It is a classic case of the right words excusing the wrong actions. It is perhaps not insignificant that some family trees show a generation of religious addiction, the following generation of alcoholism, the following of religious addiction, the following of alcoholism and so on.

Religion can be used to create a sense of control and power, for forced suppression of feelings, and as an excuse to govern the words and acts of others. It can also allow the sufferer to feel safe, through justification, from the consequences of their own actions. As with all addictions, religious addiction allows the addict to avoid dealing with reality. I have compiled the following indications of religious addiction from a number of sources.

1 Do you find that when you are faced with problems or frustrations you tend to pray or read/recite the Bible/

Talmud/Koran instead of taking an objective look at the problem and building a constructive response to it?

2 Have you changed your value system when you felt it your religious duty to do so? Have you put religion before your feelings and/or your children's feelings?

3 Are you unable to doubt or question religious information and/or authority?

4 Do you see things as black or white, good or bad?

5 Do you think that God/Allah will sort you out/do it all without serious work on your part?

6 Do you have a rigid adherence to rules, codes, ethics or guidelines? Do you often use the words 'should' or 'must'?

7 Do you readily pass judgement? Are you ready to find fault or evil?

8 Do you believe that sex is dirty and/or that physical pleasures are evil?

9 Do you overeat compulsively or fast excessively?

10 Do you put religion before science, medicine and/or education?

11 Have you alienated any family member, friend or colleague with your religious stance?

12 Have you cut back on social, family, work or other activities for your religion?

13 Do you suffer from back pains, sleeplessness, headaches, hypertension (abnormally high blood pressure)?

14 Do you manipulate scriptures or texts to justify your actions, feel specially chosen, or claim to receive messages from God/Allah?

15 Do you get into 'high' trance-like states?

If you answer 'yes' to only a few of these, you need to look at whether you are using religion to suppress your feelings and avoid dealing with reality.

OBSESSIVE-COMPULSIVE DISORDER

This consists of obsessions (repetitive thoughts) or compulsions (repetitive behaviours) which consume over an hour a day or cause noticeable distress or impairment of your ability to function. At some point, you will recognize that your actions, or those of someone close to you, are excessive or unreasonable.

Obsessive-compulsive disorders are often thought of as an addiction and do appear to be similar. But their treatment is very different from treatment for addiction, responding well to medication rather than therapy exploring possible causes. For this reason, and because they can accompany an addiction, they are detailed in Appendix II on dual disorders.

ARE YOU HAPPY?

You can use one of the checklists in this chapter to persuade a loved one into recovery – or to lead you into recovery. But a friend of mine who has a high success rate in persuading people into recovery never asks people how much they drink/drug/gamble/binge/use or how it has damaged their lives. Instead, he merely asks 'Are you happy?' As they would not be talking to him unless they needed help, the question is somewhat superfluous – but it invariably works. Then he can move on to other questions.

The next chapter shows how the addictions we have just described might have started, and how identifying some of the origins can help in the recovery process.

CHAPTER 3

'Causes'

Research into the 'causes' of addiction is still new, with discoveries being made as you read this book. Most research starts with a general knowledge of a subject, then becomes more specific. But knowledge about addiction started with a specific form – alcoholism – then expanded to include other addictions.

Effective addiction treatment on a sizeable scale began only in 1935, with Alcoholics Anonymous. Research linking alcoholism to genetic causes came as recently as 1973. It was only in the 1990s that researchers published information on the links between inheritance, chemicals in the brain and addictive behaviours.

Whilst not everyone agrees on the minutiae of the research, what is important is that there is enough to prove that addiction is not all about a lack of morals or willpower. It is not people's fault that they became addicted initially – but this book's responsibility is to show that they can recover from it.

The word 'cure' is not used, as the chemical imbalance lies dormant in recovery and can be triggered by even one reuse of the addiction.

Addiction has multiple causes and has multiple solutions. Alcoholism, the earliest addiction to be studied, has been defined as a bio-psycho-social disease/disorder. 'Bio' recognizes the tangible, chemical link. 'Psycho' indicates that it is linked with our psychology. The word 'social' is used both because alcoholism affects society and because some think that society helps to cause it. The 'disease' part still causes controversy, although the term has helped many people to recover; the word 'disorder' is becoming more popular. Let's look at all the addictions under these headings.

BIOLOGICAL OR GENETIC CAUSES

In the 1970s, research – of twins and of children separated from their parents but who turned out to have the same alcoholic characteristics – proved that alcoholism is a result of genetics rather than simply a 'learned' family trait. So children of alcoholics are more likely to become addicted than children of non-alcoholics even if they have no contact with the parent or parents.

Research published in 1995 also shows that there is a difference in one brain wave, the auditory P300, in children at risk of developing alcoholism in adulthood. This difference is not in everyone who develops alcoholism, and can 'normalize' in young adulthood, but it does not exist in children who are from non-alcoholic families.

Advances in neuroscience – the science of the brain – in the 1990s link addiction to alcohol and other substances and behaviours to a lack of certain chemicals in the brain. This helps us to see the links between the different addictions. For example, it has been found that alcohol mimics the effects of cocaine, benzodiazepines (eg Valium) and amphetamines on the brain. This is why mixing any of the above with alcohol intensifies the effect dangerously. Alcohol also resembles opium because it can trigger bodily supplies of natural morphine-like painkillers called endorphins.

In looking at how the addictions resemble each other at this level, we can also understand why treatments resemble each other. In this respect, it is worth adding that cholesterol is a complicated alcohol, which might explain some of the power of bingeing on food, and the ease of transferring addiction from one substance to another.

Understanding our brain chemistry also helps us to accept that it is vital to stay from that *first* drink, drug or other addiction which can set up the addictive chemical chain.

So . . . imagine a substance which can boost your mood, improve your memory, reduce anxiety, banish phobias, perk up your metabolism, intensify your emotions – and help you to 'just say no' to aggression, alcohol, drugs, sex, binge eating and other questionable compulsive behaviour. This is serotonin, a natural drug in your body – which is thought to be lacking, either through genetics or upbringing, in people who become addicted.

It is no wonder that people lacking serotonin turn to anything which gives the same effects which people with 'normal' biological systems automatically enjoy.

Imagine also a substance which can give you feelings ranging from a calm satiation to a mild high to euphoria and orgasm. This is dopamine, like serotonin a natural drug in your body thought to be lacking in people who become addicted.

Serotonin, dopamine and endorphins are neurotransmitters, natural chemicals in the body which transmit messages between nerve cells. The neurotransmitters affecting addiction are located in your brain's medial forebrain bundle or, to give it its more popular name, the 'pleasure pathway'.

Neurotransmitters travel only between groups of similar cells. They have many 'locks' or receptors, each interacting with a particular substance or 'key'.

Alcohol reproduces the effects of serotonin, dopamine and endorphins. Cocaine and amphetamines zero in on dopamine. Heroin, other drugs, caffeine and certain foods also behave like the neurotransmitters. The list seems to grow, with tobacco smoke being the most recent item proven to react, indirectly, with dopamine. Research has also shown that even the anticipation of alcohol raises dopamine levels. This has important implications for the craving in substance-seeking behaviour.

Research also indicates that repetitive actions can raise serotonin levels, which reinforces habit-forming behaviours.

It is thought that the amount each person possesses of these neurotransmitters is related both to their genes and their upbringing. So, in theory, both medication and/or counselling should help. But it is not as simple as it sounds. Serotonin, for example, has helped some people to stay away from alcohol – but only for a month.

The good news is that you can raise your levels of 'feel-good' chemicals yourself, and do so healthily. Many of the suggestions for recovery in Chapters 4, 5 and 6 – healthy diet, exercise, laughing, positive thoughts, relaxation, meditation and yoga – boost your serotonin levels naturally.

CAUSES FROM OUR PSYCHOLOGY AND UPBRINGING

A child with a weak serotonin/dopamine/endorphin system born into a family which provides nurture and support can do well. Sadly, children most in need of natural feelgood chemicals can be deprived of them due to the effects of abusive parenting or other trauma. Research after research, for example, has shown that a vast percentage of addicts have had an abusive childhood. This can range from shaming messages to physical and sexual abuse. And the children have not been taught 'boundaries' to protect themselves. The stage has been set for potential addiction and/or psychiatric illness.

Every alcoholic I know has talked of the 'high' and the mood change which came over them when they took their first drink. Gamblers enjoy a mood change when they bet, spenders when shopping, food addicts when bingeing or starving. Three types of addictive 'highs' have been identified: arousal and satiation are the most common, followed by fantasy which is part of all addictions. One particular substance or behaviour unlocks each addict's individual addiction-related pleasure pathway. The mood-altering experience is unforgettable. And the addict wants more.

An arousal high can come from amphetamines, cocaine, Ecstasy, the first few drinks of alcohol and from behaviours such as gambling, sex, spending and stealing. Addicts feel that they can achieve happiness, safety and fulfilment.

A satiation high can come from alcohol, heroin, marijuana, benzodiazepines and overeating. The addict feels full and complete and pain and distress are numbed. Unfortunately the feelings are only temporary.

Intellectually, addicts know that their substance or behaviour cannot fulfil them. But addiction is based on emotional logic, not intellectual logic. The substance or behaviour will 'solve' the immediate problem – giving a high or numbing pain/grief/fear – and addicts, not having been given problem-solving skills from their parents, know of no other way to solve the problem.

The situation is compounded because addicts, instead of increasing their social links naturally through problem-solving as they mature, find themselves becoming increasingly isolated.

I believe that all addiction is rooted in unresolved childhood grief or trauma. A parent or grandparent dies and the child is told not to grieve but to 'set a good example' to his/her siblings or to 'be the man/lady of the family' by not crying. 'Big boys don't cry' and 'big girls don't cry' are phrases often found in addicts' childhood messages.

Research into post-traumatic stress disorder shows that one catastrophic event in your life over which you have no control is enough to change your brain chemistry forever. Children can be sexually molested, then not believed by their parents but told to stop lying; they can be molested by their parents and blackmailed into keeping quiet. They can be beaten and told not to cry as they deserve it.

Children's traumas can come from having alcoholic parents who at the least cannot show love for them and at the worst beat or molest them. It can come from self-blame for their parents' uncaring actions, from the constant 'walking on eggshells' and emotional seesaw of their parents' unpredictability, and from the emotional blackmail addictive parents can use.

Children's grief comes from all types of loss: of a stable childhood as above; of innocence; of a loved one (through death, separation or divorce); of financial/academic/sibling status, dreams, friendships, familiar homes, pets, toys, of being believed, of self-esteem; of childhood itself – the loss of a sense of being loved, of pleasurable emotions, of an identity and of self.

Hard on the heels of unexpressed misery comes shame: 'I am bad for feeling unhappy'; 'I am not good enough to be allowed to be unhappy'; 'Unhappiness is a shameful thing'. Soon, the pain is remembered only unconsciously but the shame grows in the consciousness. And it is a terrible feeling to have to bear.

Some people commit suicide before they are fully adult. Others have a breakdown. Others turn to addiction.

Now a self-perpetuating cycle starts. The addiction is used to change shameful emotions. But being addicted and our behaviour when addicted cause more shame. The addict then seeks refuge from the pain of addiction by moving further into the addictive process. And if any adult griefs occur – such as redundancy, loss of promotion, loss of spouse – they will be suppressed in the same process, and augment and accelerate it.

Soon, all addicts need to do is think about their addiction for their mood to change. Now addicts minimize the effects of addictive behaviour – 'It's not that bad' – or forget it with the 'hair of the dog'. They distance themselves from anyone who tries to come between them and their addiction. Their behaviour worsens. They arrange their lives and relationships around their addiction.

They start to lie about their addiction, no matter how

honest they are in other areas of their lives. The food addict starts to hide food, the alcoholic to sneak in a few drinks, the gambler to open a secret bank account, the sex addict to go to prostitutes or be unfaithful.

Instead of the disciplines of a 'normal' life, there are the rituals or habits of addiction – knowing a mood-change will be there if they act in certain ways. Habits are used instead of disciplines. The daily gathering of 'drinking companions' is a habit. A bulimic's purging is a habit. A sex addict's pornography is a habit. They need to be replaced during recovery with healthier habits.

This is a terrible time for people close to the addict. They can love the true self that the addict is. But they hate the addictive personality and behaviour, the words which come out of the addict's mouth. You will have deep mood swings as the addict swiftly metamorphoses from one to the other. Your hopes rise, only to be dashed even lower. You fear the unpredictability of the addictive behaviour. You lose trust. You grieve and you feel shame. You, too, need help.

The addict, consciously or unconsciously, picks up your shame and acts out their addictive patterns even more often and in more dangerous ways. By this time, too, their tolerance for their addiction is lowering and they need more to get the same effect. Something has to break.

One day, suddenly, the addiction no longer produces the desired effect. Even the alcoholic can watch him- or herself drinking as if from the outside but no longer get drunk. Or, one day, financial ruin can stare you in the face – and this time you face up to it. The person you love most in the world threatens to leave you or has left. You are in hospital weighing only a half of what you should. You are in hospital with a sexual disease / cirrhosis of the liver / injuries from a car accident while driving under the influence of drinks or drugs or speeding to your place of addiction. You are about to be fired from your job. The social worker threatens to take your children into care.

Everyone's crisis is different – and similar in that it is an emotional rock bottom. At this stage, addicts try to do something about their addiction. Unfortunately, this usually amounts to cutting back in the mistaken belief that it can be controlled, or switching to another addiction in the mistaken belief that they can get addicted to only one thing.

It is only after using all their willpower and intellect to stay away from addiction, and having these fail miserably, that addicts turn to another source for help. This is where self-help organizations, professionals and this self-help book come in.

SOCIAL CAUSES

We live in an addictive society. We are encouraged to 'drown our sorrows' or 'have a drink to success'. Intense agony-and-ecstasy love affairs are promoted. There is widespread poverty as the gap between the 'haves' and the 'have nots' grows. And at no other time in history have mood-altering substances been so widely available.

Research on the link between availability and addiction has, as far as I know, been carried out only on alcohol. But alcohol has so far been a good marker for the other addictions. And almost all indices of alcohol-related problems are linked with annual *per capita* consumption which in turn is linked with the availability of alcohol. This has led to the suggestion that such problems are a social and political issue rather than a medical one.

For example, the fact that alcohol-related problems are linked with annual *per capita* consumption means that the more people drink in general, the more alcoholics there are likely to be. Surveys show drug-taking linked to poverty, particularly in inner cities. In both instances there is a social and cultural context.

What we need, first and foremost, is accurate information about addiction and recovery and the infrastructure to deliver it. Information such as in this book, for example, should be given to all schoolchildren – and, indeed, their families. The idea is so all-encompassing that it has frightened governments. But it starts with only one small step: the move of one addict into recovery.

CHAPTER 4

Self-Help Strategies for a Happier Life I: Emergency Tactics

The most important thing to remember when trying to give up an addiction is that it is not enough simply to say 'no'. Stopping an addiction leaves a large vacuum. And nature abhors a vacuum. This is when you can easily swap one addiction for another – unless you have some knowledge of how to fill the vacuum with healthy actions which will both get you through the short term and lay a strong foundation for the future.

Addictive behaviour takes up a lot of time. For example, if you are a gambler then, as well as the actual time spent gambling, you will have spent time travelling to races, to the betting shop, to the casino and to games arcades, and taking part in social activities which involve gambling. You will have spent much time trying to get the money to gamble, trying to find money to repay losses, avoiding creditors, and making excuses to friends, family and employer (if you have them left).

If you are a shopaholic, you can pass days at a time going round the shops. If you are a sex addict, you can while away time reading pornographic magazines, inviting potential sexual partners to dinner and preparing for that, dressing up to meet them elsewhere, 'cruising' for potential partners and planning your sexual activity. Time is spent both in the repetitive actions and in your mind's preoccupation.

If you are an alcoholic, you will have spent time travelling to different off-licences so that you will not seem to be visiting any one too frequently, you will have gone to social events where you can drink, you will have spent whole evenings in the pub – and nights and days sleeping off the effects. You might even have served time in police cells as a result.

If you are a drug addict, you will also have wasted time sleeping off the effects of your drugs, as well as visiting different doctors trying to get multiple prescriptions, visiting different chemists for each prescription, and maybe shoplifting, mugging or burgling to finance your habit. Selling on those goods takes time. Meeting up with a dealer takes time.

If you are a food addict, you can can also pass time at social occasions where you can eat unnoticed, or you can spend time stealing away and hiding food to eat in private, making excuses to others for your absence. You spend hours throwing up. You might browse around healthfood shops or slave over the oven. You might spend much time exercising, which is part of some food addictions.

So what things would it be helpful to fill your time with? It is probably best to divide self-help into two headings: help for emergencies, detailed in this chapter, and longer-term strategies which are described in the following two chapters. Get to know the emergency tactics first so that if at any time you feel overwhelmed with despair, rage, helplessness, pain, sadness or any other emotion – including boredom – you can get some immediate ease from these tactics rather than turning back to your addiction.

EMERGENCY TACTICS

In all the following suggestions, you are asked to concentrate on an action, by the end of which your cravings or overwhelming feelings should have reduced or even disappeared. Remember that cravings and feelings do *not* last, even though it may not feel that way at the time. They are impermanent. The trick is to occupy yourself until they go away.

1 Breathe deeply and slowly

This sounds too simple to be true, but it can bring immediate results. Many people do not breathe deeply enough even though shallow breathing raises levels of the body's stress hormones, leading to constriction of blood vessels and tension in the heart. Focus your mind on your breathing so that it flows freely and deeply. This will give you some calm. Blow into a paper bag if necessary, or into your cupped hands if you don't have one – science proves that it is calming to inhale the exhaled air.

The following methods of relaxed breathing are taken from another book in this series, *Anxiety, Phobias and Panic Attacks* by Elaine Sheehan. They are based on techniques by Beta Jencks.

Long breath

Keeping your shoulders still, imagine inhaling through the fingertips, up the arms and into the shoulders, then exhaling down the trunk into the abdomen and legs and out of the toes. Repeat.

Breathing through the skin

Imagine inhaling and exhaling through the skin on any part of your body. On each inhalation, allow the skin to feel refreshed and invigorated. On each exhalation, permit the skin to relax.

Abdominal breathing

Place your hands over the area around your navel and focus your attention there. Begin inhaling deeply, expanding your stomach as much as possible so that your hands rise gently. Now exhale, taking twice as long as you did to inhale, pulling your abdomen muscles in and noticing the fall of the hands. Repeat.

Imagined agent

As you breathe, imagine you are inhaling a bronchodilator agent which relaxes and widens the walls of the air paths in the bronchi and lungs, allowing the air to stream in easily. As you exhale, notice the soft collapse of these air passages. Repeat.

Waves or tides

Lie on your back. For two or three respiratory cycles, imagine that your breath is flowing with ocean waves or tides. Feel the passive flowing in and out.

2 Let five minutes pass before you act

3 Telephone someone you trust

This may be harder than it sounds as your 'friends' may be people who drink/drug/gamble/binge/behave addictively, and your family might not know what to do. But it is surprising how many people whom you might have regarded as mere acquaintances turn out to be pure gold. Telephone someone you admire for getting their lives together, telephone people who are recovering from any addiction, telephone the 12–step or self-help group for your addiction, telephone your therapist if you have one, even telephone the Samaritans – you don't have to be suicidal to talk to them. The miracle is that, when you share your feelings or cravings with someone else, they usually disappear.

Remember: most people like to feel useful, and you give them the gift of feeling useful when you ask for help.

If the first person you call is not in, leave a message on their answerphone, then try calling 10 more people. Even if you do not reach anyone, by the time you have finished dialling the craving will have diminished or disappeared.

Make a written note of your feelings the first few times after you talk to someone. Did you feel better after each call? You might want to cross some people off your list. And beware if you feel grateful to someone for bothering with you: you don't need to talk to people who leave you feeling you're not as good as them. List the people who leave you feeling better about yourself.

4 Meet someone to talk to

Meet a trustworthy friend at home or a place where you cannot indulge in your addiction. If you cannot talk about your feelings, talk about anything else. If your craving was triggered by a specific problem, try to talk honestly about it. Ask not to be left alone.

5 Do something that makes you feel good

Distract yourself by playing music, having a luxurious bath, doing the washing, cleaning out your wardrobe, painting a wall, reading a gripping book. Or leave the house and go somewhere safe where you cannot relapse into your addiction – a drive in the country, a film, a museum. By the time you've finished, the craving should have gone.

6 Go to a meeting

If there is a 12–step or other self-help meeting for your particular addiction, go to it. Some groups will arrange for you to be picked up if it is your first time (*see* Chapter 7).

7 Keep your feelgood factory open

Remind yourself that relapsing will devastate your body's natural production of chemicals to make you feel good (*see* Chapter 3), that it will be replaced by a process in your body which leads to addiction and depression. Your uncomfortable feelings will last for a much shorter time than any addiction the process starts.

8 Remind yourself of past experiences

Remind yourself of the most shaming things which happened to you while you were using. Remind yourself of how you hurt not only yourself but those you love and respect. Then think of how much you want to regain their trust.

9 Write down worst-case scenarios

Write down all the bad things that will happen if you give in. After all, why should this time be any better than past experience?

10 Meditate

Focus your mind on a pleasant image. Buy relaxation or 'guided-meditation' tapes to make this even easier. Buy and read a 'daily meditation' book which has an uplifting thought for every day of the year. Browsing through a bookshop looking for these can be a meditation in itself!

The health benefits of meditation, including lowering of blood pressure, have been confirmed by over 500 scientific studies. Visualize how you would like your life to change.

11 Have a laugh

Dr Robert Holden, who once ran a laughter clinic in the UK, advises everyone to sit cross-legged in front of a mirror each morning and laugh for two minutes for no reason whatsoever!

12 Read recovery literature

Get hold of some literature on recovery from your addiction, if you haven't already done so, and read it. Listen to a recovery tape or video. If there is a dearth of recovery materials in your area, get hold of some on self-esteem, visualization, relaxation techniques, and the like.

13 Write a gratitude list

It may sound pious, but it can be a very quick fix. Just write down everything for which you are grateful at this moment, no matter how small.

14 Write an anger list

If you are raging, write an anger list. Don't think. Just write down as quickly as possible everything which angers you, from dirty carpets to downright tragedy. I guarantee that this will not make you more angry – in fact, your anger will change.

15 Eat

Have a snack, preferably one which is low in sugar. Drink natural fruit juices and mineral water.

If your addiction is related to food, avoid so-called 'trigger foods'. These are usually reminiscent of childhood treats and usually refined-sugar based or dairy produce like cream and cheese; they can trigger you into bingeing on almost anything. Avoidance of trigger foods can be reinforced with a healthy three-meals-a-day diet.

16 Treat yourself – you're worth it

Take the money you are thinking of spending on your addiction (unless you are a compulsive spender) and spend it on an on-the-spot treat for yourself, or put it in a piggy bank for a future treat.

17 Halt

Don't get hungry, angry, lonely or tired. You will only become more vulnerable.

DETOXIFICATION

If you or someone close to you has been using chemicals to excess, a supervised withdrawal or 'detoxification' – in which your body rids itself of the toxic substances – might be necessary. This is not a treatment. It will not keep you clean or sober. But it will get the poisons out of your body so that you can start on the road to recovery.

It is important to check with a doctor before withdrawing from your drug of choice, as withdrawal can be dangerous – it depends on how much and what you have been using. A 'detox' can be carried out at home under the supervision of a visiting doctor or nurse, in hospital or in a treatment centre.

Withdrawal symptoms can range from slightly uncomfortable to painful, to fits, and even to death if unsupervised. Medication is sometimes necessary.

Some drugs, such as alcohol, are flushed out of your system in a few days. Marijuana can take weeks. After stopping Valium it can take years for symptoms such as panic attacks to disappear.

How do you know when a detox is needed? These are some of the signs:

- hallucinations
- difficulty breathing
- seizure
- unconsciousness
- sudden chest or abdominal pain
- violent behaviour or risk of violent behaviour
- DTs – delirium tremens (convulsion, trembling and hallucinations as a result of alcohol)
- temperature over 102°F (39°C)
- pulse over 120 beats/minute
- vomiting/vomiting of blood.

CHAPTER 5

Self-Help Strategies for a Happier Life II: Solid Base for Long-Term Plans

You can recover without self-esteem. You cannot recover without boundaries.

PIA MELLODY
codependency pioneer, author, lecturer

The most important strategy for long-term emotional health – for anyone, not just addicts – is to learn about, and practise using, 'boundaries'. Once your boundaries are in place, it is easier to use all the other strategies and to withstand pressures from people tempting you back to an addictive way of life. They also lead to much more rewarding and fulfilling relationships with other people.

Boundaries exist to protect us from hurt – be it emotional, physical or sexual. When we know what they are, they also prevent us from accidentally hurting other people because they can now feel safe and comfortable in our company. We gain self-esteem from knowing this.

So what is a boundary? Think of the boundary of a country. It prevents people coming and going as they please – but there are passport controls through which people can pass once their credentials have been checked. This system exists to protect the country and its inhabitants.

If there were no boundaries around the country, it could

be invaded by hostile armies. If there were only walls around the country, such as the old Berlin Wall separating East and West Germany, no one could get in – but no one could get out, either. The fortress becomes a prison.

Most addicts are like this: having no walls so that they have no protection from damaging people or substances, or surrounding themselves with walls through which no one can communicate with them and through which they cannot communicate with others. They have not even conceived the idea of a check-in zone.

The story below comes from someone who built walls around himself. He was cut off from anyone who could help him – and from those he loved and by whom he wished to be loved.

I liked to look self-sufficient, as if I needed no one. I had been taught as a child that that meant I looked successful. I did this very well.

My wall of self-sufficiency meant that no one could see that I needed help. I had no walls with my long-term partner, who hit out at me on a regular basis, sometimes with a knife, and gave me put-downs almost constantly. I drank so as not to feel this, then became so dependent on the drink numbing me that I had all the problems associated with anyone who drinks daily, including the possibility of losing my job and thus my mortgage and home. But I couldn't tell anyone. Ridiculous as it seems now, I feared what they might say more than the hellish reality of my situation.

When I at last broke through the wall between me and other people and asked for help, it was such a relief! And everyone treated me with so much more kindness than I could ever have expected. For the first time in seven years, my situation changed.

SEAN

My own story below is typical of someone without walls. Almost everything everyone said to me hurt, and threw me more and more into my addiction to escape the hurt as I knew no other way of dealing with it.

*Before recovery, if people criticized me, I always believed them. Even
if what they said wasn't true, I thought I must be wrong. On the
rare occasions I knew they were wrong, I desperately justified myself
to my 'critics'. I always tried to change myself to suit them, so that
they would say nice things. In the end, most people did say nice
things (except about my addiction!) but it was almost constant work,
anticipation and worry.*

*Worse – as I got into recovery, people told me that I was getting
angry and reacting to comments that were not meant as criticisms.
To me, they were. I had to learn to tell the difference.*

*More importantly, did it matter what others thought? This was
an earth-shattering idea for me. I had never asked myself that question. Did what they said matter? This boundary question was a big
turning point.*

*At the stage when almost everything said to me hurt, I attacked
or defended without thinking. My tongue was quicker than my
thoughts. Now I have learned – slowly – to keep quiet, ask myself
whether the comment is true (I can tell much better now), and
whether it matters; then I decide what I want to say – or not say. I
am rarely hurt. There are few arguments. Usually, I gain a lot of
self-esteem. These 'boundaries' are probably the most important ones
I have learned.*

DEIRDRE

When should you use your boundaries? When you need
to protect your rights as a human being and when you
feel pushed or pulled back into addictive behaviour. Most
addicts were never taught their rights as human beings,
so some of these are listed below (from *Boundaries and
Relationships: Knowing, Protecting and Enjoying the Self* by
Dr Charles Whitfield).

MY RIGHTS AS A HUMAN BEING

1 I have the right to grieve over what I did not get that I
  needed and what I got that I did not need or want.
2 I have the right to follow my own values and standards.
3 I have the right to say no to anything when I feel I am
  not ready, it is unsafe or it violates my values.

4 I have the right to dignity and respect.

5 I have the right to make decisions based on my feelings, my judgement or any reason that I choose.

6 I have the right to set and honour my own priorities.

7 I have the right to have my needs and wants respected by others.

8 I have the right to terminate conversations with people by whom I feel put down and humiliated.

9 I have the right not to be responsible for others' behaviours, actions, feelings or problems.

10 I have the right to make mistakes and not have to be perfect.

11 I have the right to expect honesty from others.

12 I have the right to all my feelings.

13 I have the right to be angry with someone I love.

14 I have the right to be uniquely me, without feeling that I am not good enough.

15 I have the right to feel scared and to say 'I am afraid'.

16 I have the right to experience and then let go of fear, guilt and shame.

17 I have the right to change my mind at any time.

18 I have the right to be happy.

19 I have the right to my own personal space and time.

20 I have the right to be relaxed, playful and frivolous.

21 I have the right to change and grow.

22 I have the right to improve my communication skills so that I may be understood.

23 I have the right to make friends and be comfortable with people.

24 I have the right to be in a nonabusive environment.

25 I have the right to be healthier than those around me.

26 I have the right to take care of myself, no matter what.

27 I have the right to grieve over actual or threatened losses.

28 I have the right to trust others who earn my trust.

29 I have the right to give and receive unconditional love.

USING BOUNDARIES

I visualize my boundaries as being like the force-field around the Starship Enterprise. It can be as wide or as narrow as I like and I can switch it on or off at will, instantly or gradually; I prefer this flexibility to the idea of a country's boundaries. It can deflect anything harmful, chance meteor storm, enemy weapons or ill-wishers – yet I can beam on board anything I like. It gives physical, emotional and perhaps sexual boundaries.

And if I'm not certain about someone or something, I can beam them aboard but ask the crew to watch them. That is what I can do with ideas, comments, criticism – anything, in fact, that enters my life nowadays. My force-field protects me so well that sometimes I am unconscious of it working.

Physical boundaries

I also set other, physical boundaries about where I take my 'starship'. For example, I used to fall for violent alcoholic men who caused me so much pain that I do not wish to repeat the experiences. If I do not set course for a pub, then the odds are lowered that I will meet another such alcoholic. The pub door is a physical boundary which I will not pass. I do not even have to think about any sexual or emotional boundaries, as maintaining the physical one automatically protects these.

Of course, not passing a pub/disco/casino/sweet-shop door is also a physical boundary for someone trying to give up alcohol/drugs/gambling/bingeing. If they do not pass through this physical boundary, they also will not have to face the persuasions of their addictive companions to join them (emotional boundary).

Changing your playpen – and your playmates – as above, is a very good way of using boundaries to help keep you away from your addiction.

Emotional boundaries

The 'cracked record' technique usually now comes into play, as your old playmates try to persuade you – and they will try, believe me – to relapse. This technique is based on the *right* which we all have to say 'no' without an excuse. If you feel that you must make an excuse, think of only one and stick to that, repeating it, if necessary, like a cracked record. This will save you trying to find answers or justify yourself to invidious persuasions. It makes saying 'no' to protect yourself much easier.

I was scared stiff of returning to my house to pick up some clothes, while I was staying with some good friends to try and sort out my addiction. My neighbour tended to come in when she wanted (once, she appeared in my bedroom at 6 am) and to throw tantrums. I didn't think I could face her, especially when I had only recently admitted to my addiction. She would use it against me.

I was shocked to be told that my front door was a boundary! That I had a right not to let anyone through it that I did not want!

'But she'll say this, she'll say that,' I complained. She could manipulate any excuse I could give. I was told to reply simply, 'I can't let you in now'.

'What!' I shrieked. I'd never get away with that.

'If you must give an excuse, say "I can't let you in now, I have things to do". Don't say anything else. Just repeat that one sentence like a broken record: "I can't let you in now, I have things to do". And don't be tempted to explain what things.'

I spent half a day at my house and my neighbour did not turn up. But I spent my travel time and my time in the house muttering 'I can't let you in now, I have things to do' – and I was relaxed and unworried. I knew that I had a tool to deal with her – and was (almost) looking forward to her arrival. It ended up being a rewarding day, and I felt good for a long time afterwards.

BRYAN

My earliest knowledge of boundaries came from addiction

counsellor Sally Benjamin, who now practises in the south of England. She describes a similar example of how feelings can signal the need for boundaries.

> Your neighbour keeps dropping in unannounced. You like her but are beginning to feel irritated: you wish she would ring first but are afraid to tell her for fear of offending her. Then she wouldn't want to be friends with you any more; anyway, she will probably stop when the decorators are finished in her house.
>
> What is happening here? First, your irritation (a reaction to your instinctual knowledge that you are being invaded) is dismissed. The neighbour's feelings, which you have imagined you know, are deemed to be more important than your own. (This is an invasion of the neighbour's boundaries, by the way. Did she give you permission to decide what she should feel?) The forecast for the relationship is poor, based again on what you predict your neighbour's reaction will be. You have cast her as a shallow, hypersensitive, unfeeling and selfish person *without checking* with her the basis for your judgement.
>
> The one thing you will have predicted accurately is what will eventually happen if you do not set your boundary and ask her to ring before coming over. Your mild irritation will surely grow, creating an explosion which will probably end the friendship. The neighbour won't know what hit her, and you will feel angry with yourself and guilty for overreacting, shame for your cowardice in not speaking up earlier, and unconscious guilt for the boundary invasion to start with. This is not a recipe for self-esteem.
>
> Then you will apologize, without really knowing what you are apologizing for. You have again not set a boundary and are setting the scene for a re-run.

You are also setting the scene for a relapse. These are feelings on which people drink/drug/eat/relapse – but are avoidable if you set the boundary. It becomes a straight-forward choice: boundary or relapse into addiction?

PHYSICAL BOUNDARY STATEMENT
'I have the right to control
distance from and non-sexual touching with you
and you have the same right with me.'

SEXUAL BOUNDARY STATEMENT
'I have the right to determine
with whom, when, where and how
I will be sexual.'

**INTERNAL BOUNDARY STATEMENT/
EMOTIONAL BOUNDARY STATEMENT**
'I create what I think and feel and
I choose to do (or not do) what I do (or do not do);
and you do the same.'

Pia Mellody
From her videotape *Codependency*

SETTING BOUNDARIES

Here are some examples of boundary use.

- Is that accusation true?
- If not, what do I want to do?
- If true, do I care?
- I will not give my telephone number to him/her.
- I will/will not allow him/her through my front/sitting-room/bedroom door.
- I will not accept calls after, say, 11pm – even from friends.
- I will not allow my colleague to take credit for my work.
- I will allow a hug but not a kiss.
- I'll stay a mile away from him/her!
- I will not allow my sister to call me fat/stupid/unkind.
- I will not go to a pub/dealer/bookmakers.

- Accepting a dinner invitation does not mean going to bed.
- Dancing with someone does not mean having sex.
- I will not drink/drug/binge/gamble or otherwise behave addictively.
- I will not go out with addictive people.
- I will protect my rights as a human being.

If you have a difficult situation to deal with, it can be useful to write down beforehand what you want to say and even to try it out on an understanding friend who will give you an objective opinion. In cases where there is a lot of fear, it might help to have a friend stay with you as you make the call or face the person involved. Usually these situations are the result of having put up with boundary violations over too long a period of time. The build-up of anger generates fear – of what will come out of your mouth, of the other person's reaction. And there is no more paralysing emotion.

A useful exercise before you start saying 'no'

The following is a useful exercise, devised by Sally Benjamin, before you start saying 'no'. Having first identified that a boundary needs to be set, answer the following questions.

- What boundary is needed (physical, sexual, emotional)?
- Why do I want it?
- Could this boundary be damaging – to myself? to others?
- How is it useful – to myself? to others?
- How could it be lost?
- What would be the results of that loss – to myself? to others?
- How can it be maintained?
- What would be the results of maintaining it – for myself? for others?

If all these questions are thoroughly answered, it will become clear whether the boundary you are considering is the correct one, and if it will serve the purpose you intend without creating too much havoc. It is possible to set unnecessary or wrong boundaries because of fear of setting the one we need to.

Remember that boundaries should be flexible. Sometimes compromises are necessary, but never at the expense of your peace of mind. And never at the expense of your recovery.

Remember, too, to keep your boundaries. To insist on a boundary one day and dismiss it the next will create an atmosphere of confusion and fear that will lead to trouble. Many addicts have childhood memories of punishment for breaking 'unspoken rules' – one day it is OK to do a certain thing, the next it is not – and, indeed, have fears in adult relationships of breaking their partners' unspoken rules. Not to keep a boundary has the same effect of making people walk on eggshells around you, feeling uncomfortable about your unpredictable reactions.

It can be tempting to set boundaries in all areas of your life at once, particularly if you have had an initial success. Don't. In the first place, boundary-setting is a very uncomfortable, sometimes painful, business. After all, in most cases, you are changing the patterns of a lifetime. The people with whom you are setting boundaries will not be happy with you initially (it is only initially). You will be telling them they cannot do something they have been accustomed to doing, perhaps for years. Don't panic.

They will not reject you. But, unless they are exceptional people, they will not smile at you and tell you how happy they are that you have set your boundary – particularly if you are not going to support their own addictions by joining in with them. They will argue and manipulate but eventually, if you stick to it, they will capitulate.

The ten commandments of risk-taking

Finally, setting a boundary is a risk. The bigger the risk, the bigger the reward – but also the bigger the fear. Irene McMahon Cummings has listed ten 'commandments' of risk-taking and these can give comfort if you read them before taking a risk.

1 Thou shalt know that all growth requires risk.
2 Thou shalt access all options.
3 Thou shalt be willing to look foolish and feel uncomfortable.
4 Thou shalt seek emotional support.
5 Thou shalt be willing to pay the price.
6 Thou shalt know that it is OK to change your mind.
7 Thou shalt know that being rejected is not the worst thing that will ever happen to you!
8 Thou shalt be willing to be without answers.
9 Thou shalt know that if you don't try, you will never know.
10 Thou shalt acknowledge, in the very deepest part of your being, that life is precious and all too short. Trust yourself . . . Listen to your heart.

CHAPTER 6

Self-Help Strategies for a Happier Life III: Long-Term Plans

What you have to do to make a successful recovery from any disease (cancer, heart disease, alcoholism, addiction) is usually not fun, but it is often necessary for survival.

AL MOONEY, ARLENE AND HOWARD EISENBERG

Actually, some of the things you can do to recover from addiction are fun. And even some of the more difficult actions leave you feeling better about yourself afterwards. Others might leave you with mixed feelings or with uncomfortable or painful feelings which take a while to leave – but they do leave. Working at recovery is not all blood and sweat; there can be much enjoyment.

One of the most important elements of recovery is peer-support self-help groups, usually '12-Step groups'. Chapter 7 is devoted to an explanation of what they are and how they work.

If you wish to consolidate the help and support you are gaining from these groups – or if you cannot get to any – there are many other positive steps which you can take to help you recover from addiction. Those described in this chapter are all complementary to each other, so you can pick and mix as you like: try all or just a few. The more you do the better you will feel.

You will get even more out of these techniques if you accompany them with *counselling*. How to choose a counsellor and what to expect are described in Chapter 8.

One day at a time – or even one minute or one hour at a time – is all you need to think about. Do not project into the future: look after your recovery a day at a time and it will build your future. Keep everything in the day. If you can't do anything about a situation today, don't worry about it today. Similarly, if you cannot do anything about a past event, don't worry about it. There is a wonderful phrase which goes 'If you have one foot in the past and one foot in the future, you are in an excellent position to s--t on the present'.

Don't forget to breathe properly, meditate and have a laugh, as recommended in Chapter 4. They are all excellent tools to help you 'stay in the present'. Practise all these daily, not just in emergencies. There are many books, tapes and courses on breathing and meditation, usually found under the 'holistic health', 'self-help' or 'popular psychology' sections of bookshops. All these will help to ease you through difficult times.

One very effective – and enjoyable – help in early recovery is *acupuncture.* Choose your practitioner from a registered accreditation list and ask if any specialize in addiction recovery. This small number of specialists is growing as the power of acupuncture in addiction recovery is recognized; some are now attached to doctors' clinics and to hospitals.

Acupuncture sometimes takes place in a group setting so that nervous newcomers can see that the treatment does not hurt. For addiction, needles can be inserted into the ear lobes to stimulate the liver and kidneys. They are usually left in for between 20 to 40 minutes and are, perhaps surprisingly, not painful.

As well as addressing physical damage, needles can be put in at the top of your head to allow endorphins – and serotonin – to flow. This particular aspect of acupuncture can produce a feeling of euphoria or floating when first experienced – wonderful! This also helps to reduce cravings, giving physical and emotional relief to sufferers.

Because it reduces or eliminates the need for medication

during detoxification, acupuncture is usually safe for pregnant women.

Another good start to your recovery is a *supplement of vitamin B* from your doctor or healthfood shop. This is vital in rebuilding your nervous system and is your body's natural antidepressant, this having been removed from your system by alcohol and other drugs. Not only will you feel better and have fewer cravings but you will notice that all those bruises which result from mood-altering chemicals eating away at your vitamin B are starting to disappear! This, too, helps to make you feel good about yourself.

Don't procrastinate – do whatever you need to do now, be it getting out of bed, telephoning a friend, going to a meeting or going for a walk. You will only feel guilty if you put things off. *Plan one accomplishment for the day.*

Consider hormones. Many women are unaware of the impact of premenstrual, menstrual or menopausal symptoms – until they come into recovery. Newcomers to recovery often have volatile mood swings and these can be worsened at certain times of the month, when the smallest of negative feelings can be magnified. You or your therapist might search for psychological reasons for moods when in fact they are due to a hormone imbalance.

Start a diary showing when menstruation occurs and dating your negative feelings. You will probably see a link. You might notice that you eat more sugary foods on a monthly cycle also. *Evening primrose oil capsules* can help to even out your hormones and mood swings, as can a balanced diet.

If this does not help, and your mood swings do show a link to menstrual or menopausal symptoms, ask your doctor for a hormone indicator test. There are risks associated with hormone treatment, so you must discuss them with your doctor and balance these risks against the risk of relapse.

Don't try to make amends too soon. Many people, when they first stop using their addiction, feel an impulse to share inappropriate explanations or promises with their family and perhaps colleagues and friends. Don't! If you relapse, you will have raised false hopes and they will not trust you again so easily. In fact, most people will have already promised something on similar lines so often in the past that there is no reason for anyone to believe them this time. Trust is gained over time. The longer you stay in remission from your addiction, the more people will automatically – without your trying to persuade them – trust you.

Many people I know are still making amends years later for the so-called 'amends' they made in their first flush of recovery. They shocked those close to them by revealing emotions they could not deal with, by talking about child-hood abuse of which they were not aware, by disclosing past affairs, and projecting shame about deeds undertaken in active addiction. Be aware that your judgement is con-fused at this time. But your timing and prudence can be excellent if you wait.

Don't worry about dreams in which you use your addiction, particularly if they have a bad ending. Our dreams are a way in which we explore possibilities we have consciously or unconsciously been considering. It is much safer to relapse in a dream and wake up with the awful conse-quences than it is to do so in real life! If you have a using dream with a bad ending, you are less likely to repeat the actions in reality.

Affirmations are also good for you. Write down three positive facts about yourself on a small piece of paper and stick it on the mirror you look into every morning. Say them out loud. Include the sentence 'I love you' as you stare at your reflection.

If you cannot think of three positive facts about yourself, ask a friend. Even if you feel that what you are writing or saying is a lie, do it. Your unconscious hears *everything* you tell it and, having no judgement, takes it in as fact. Eventually, you will consciously accept that these affir-mations about you are true.

Add more affirmations to your list as you become aware of them.

Because you might have been insulted or put down in the first, second and third person, it helps to say and write the affirmations in the first, second and third person also. For example, someone affirms that you are a kind person, so you say:

'I, [your name], am a kind person.'
'You, [your name], are a kind person.'
'She, [your name], is a kind person.' '[your name] is a kind person.'

Affirmations might not bring instant results (or they might, if the friends you ask surprise you nicely with their affirmations of you) but they do work. They adjust your image of yourself to a more accurate, positive picture.

Now it is time for some tough work. Remember when doing some of the following exercises that your addiction did not develop instantly and so you will not get better instantly. Be a kind taskmaster to yourself – would you ask of someone else what you are now asking of yourself? Each week, you should feel a little better than the week before. Don't expect perfection – *expect progress in the right direction*. And remember that all human beings have a *right* to make mistakes.

Remember, too, that progress is slower for people who have been on cocaine or long-lasting drugs like Valium and the benzodiazepines. But everyone who sticks with a recovery programme makes progress.

To see your progress more positively, and to reduce your mood swings, *take a daily inventory* by writing down, just before you go to bed, the good and bad points of the day. If there are more of the latter than the former, add some of the following to the plus side:

'My intentions were good.'
'I tried.'
'I was willing.'
'I did not drink/drug/gamble/sex/otherwise relapse.'

You will always, somehow, find that the pluses outweigh the minuses. And you can usually correct some of the minuses the next day. This list, no matter how simple it sounds, manages to balance the emotions as easily as it balances the pluses and minuses.

Talking of the long-lasting effects of drugs, *see a doctor* to check your health. Reality will turn out to be much better than your fears. And many illnesses resulting from addiction are curable. Even the liver can repair itself. You deserve to have your body looked after. Also, addiction is about avoiding reality, so facing up to this reality gives the addiction less of an excuse to come back.

If your own doctor does not understand about addiction, ask an organization such as the Medical Council on Alcoholism in the UK or the American Society of Addiction Medicine for a doctor in your area who understands about, and is sympathetic to, recovery from addiction.

Ask for help when you need it: from members of your self-help group, from trusted friends, from your therapist, from other professionals.

Don't make excuses or give a life story when saying 'no' if people invite you to drink/drug/gamble/binge or otherwise relapse into your addiction. Simply say 'I'm not drinking / drugging / gambling / sexing [name your addictive behaviour] *tonight'*. People are less prompted to ask you for reasons you might find embarrassing if you say it is only for 'today' or 'tonight' than that you have given up permanently. If someone continues to press you, they have a problem themselves.

Practise the 'cracked record' technique described in Chapter 5 before you go to any event or take any telephone call in which you think people might encourage you to relapse.

Write a goodbye letter to your addiction. Say how much it has meant to you but explain how it has destroyed your life and why you need to part in order to move on. If you write genuinely, I guarantee that this will help you to accept the loss of your addiction.

After writing the letter, you might want to read it aloud to a trusted friend or therapist, to reinforce its message and allow the feelings to come out. Remember that feelings which come out of your body are, by definition, no longer inside you to disturb you.

If in doubt about whether you have written a genuine goodbye letter, check the 'solutions' at the end of this chapter.

EXAMINING CHILDHOOD MESSAGES

Change your thinking. The world will not change around you but your attitude to it can become less fearful, more confident, more trusting and generally happier. The first step is to *examine your childhood messages* and 'reprogramme' them like obsolete computer software.

For some people, this is a calm step forward. For others, it involves pain, anger or grief. Working through my childhood messages has probably been the single most important factor in building my self-esteem and is the force behind changing maybe 95 per cent of my previously destructive behaviour. But it does involve risk, because you cannot predict what emotions you will feel when doing this exercise.

A few years ago I asked some people to work on the meanings behind their childhood messages. Some needed to have positive and supportive people around them to talk through their reactions and come out the other side feeling stronger and freer. For one or two, this took a week and their self-esteem plummeted temporarily in that time. My own reaction was rage, but the exercise has built self-esteem for the long term.

Before you start the exercise, telephone one or two trusted, healthy people. If at any stage you find yourself in distress, telephone them again. If necessary, contact a therapist for a consultation.

To start, divide a page into two columns. Fill the left-hand one with every childhood message that occurs to you, up to about two dozen. Don't analyse. Don't think. Just write as the messages arise in your memory. Give yourself ten minutes to do this, then pause (you can always add some more later). Mark the six which you feel most strongly about – it does not matter what the feeling is, just that it is a strong one. Don't read any further until you have done this.

Well done! It takes courage and honesty to write down your childhood messages. It is also another step in building your recovery, by showing that you value yourself enough to do this exercise.

Liz's messages	*Interpretation*
Be good Don't answer back Don't argue with me You never listen to advice	Do what I tell you, without question
Wait till your father gets home All you ever do is cry When I was your age I had to . . . I never had the advantages you had	If you don't, the threats will worsen . . . and I'll put you down . . . or emotionally blackmail you
You are not like – – – Why can't you be more like – – – You can't have that	You are not good enough
We are not like them We can't keep up with them	. . . because we are not good enough
You're not going out like that!	You don't look good enough
Don't tell about – – –	Don't check the facts or work through your pain by talking with someone
Look what you're doing to us	All this is your fault, not ours You're not good enough You are ungrateful

The left-hand column contains childhood messages written

by 'Liz' when she was about two years into recovery. My interpretations are in the right-hand column. Liz then took the most important step: replacing the original messages with positive ones, which is what the right-hand column on your own page is for.

The reason for marking the six most memorable messages is that they usually combine to form a single, particularly strong message. This is probably the message which most influences your low opinion of yourself. Then ask yourself 'Were they right?' The answer is a resounding 'no'!

Before you compare your messages with Liz's, and start replacing them with positive *accurate* ones, glance at these childhood rules and messages compiled by Dr Charles Whitfield in his bestseller *Healing the Child Within*. In recognizing some of them you will know that you are not alone and you can start shedding them. You did not deserve these messages.

Negative rules and messages commonly heard in troubled families

Negative rules

Don't express feelings
Don't get upset
Do as I say, not as I do
Do well in school
Don't betray the family
Be seen and not heard!
Don't talk back
Don't discuss the family with outsiders; keep the family secret
Don't think or talk; just follow directions
Always maintain the status quo.

Don't get angry
Don't cry
Be good, 'nice', perfect
Don't ask questions
Always look good
Always be in control
Don't contradict me
Avoid conflict (or avoid dealing with conflict)
I'm always right, you're always wrong
Drinking (or other troubled behaviour) is not the cause of our problems

Focus on the alcoholic's
drinking (or troubled person's
behaviour) instead of my/
your problems

Negative messages

Shame on you
I wish I'd never had you
Be dependent
Big boys don't cry
Act like a nice girl (or lady)
You're so stupid (or bad etc)

You caused it
Of course we love you!
I'm sacrificing myself for you
We won't love you if you . . .
You'll never accomplish
anything
It didn't really hurt
I promise [though breaks it]
You're so stupid
You _____ [rude name]!

You're not good enough
Hurry up and grow up
Be a man
You don't feel that way
Don't be like that
Your needs are not all right
with me
You owe it to us
How can you do this to me?
You're so selfish
You're driving me mad!
You'll be the death of me

That's not true
You make me sick!
We wanted a boy/girl

Recognize anything? These messages are as wrong now as
when you were a child, and just as wrong for other
children. Note that the messages are compounded by
'rules' which forbid the healthy, healing expression of feelings. So we learn that we are bad, and that we are not to
talk about any of it.

It might help to know that parents *pass on what they have
experienced themselves*. They pass on the messages given to
them by your grandparents, who were given them by your
great-grandparents, and so on up the line. Many parents
still live with the pain of their own messages, and are
unaware of their damaging effect. You are breaking a long
generational chain, and starting your own dynastic line!

Reprogramming

The following are some examples of 'reprogramming'.

Old Message	*New Message*
Put others first Family hold back	Everyone is equal – including me I have equal rights with any other human being
Self-praise is no praise	True humility is accepting myself as I am, good as well as bad
You're not good enough	I am perfect at being me I am perfectly me
I can't get this perfect	I can do an excellent job
You're bad for making mistakes	I have a *right* to make mistakes
You're stupid for making mistakes You should have known	Who taught me?

Many people's addictions accelerate as they distance themselves from a god/divine being/higher power. *Gaining hope of being reconnected to a healing higher power* helps the recovery process enormously. Again, that loss of hope has usually started not in the addictive behaviour but from childhood messages.

> *'Don't do that; God will punish you.' This message, received from many people, distorted my relationship with God. He was someone to fear and avoid at all costs. Instead of seeking him for support and guidance, I tried to distance myself so God could not see my mistakes and imperfections. This played into my perfectionism: no matter how hard I tried, it was not good enough – I was unworthy. As an adult, I have turned this message around in a variety of ways: 'I am a growing and developing person – it is OK to make mistakes on my journey' and 'God loves me unconditionally as I am His child'.*

JERRY MOE
Director, Sierra Tucson Children's Programme
Vice-president, National Association for Children of Alcoholics

CHANGING ANY DISTORTED THINKING

Consolidate your work on childhood messages by looking at your current thinking. As your interpretations of the events around you change, so do your mood and attitude.

An assessment of your distorted thinking styles takes several days, as you observe your thinking in a variety of stress situations. The *habit* of combating the distortions will take from two weeks to several months to become automatic.

15 styles of distorted thinking

The following list of styles of distorted thinking was compiled by Mathew McKay, Martha Davis and Patrick Fanning in their book *Thoughts & Feelings: The Art of Cognitive Stress Intervention*.

Filtering

You take the negative details and magnify them while filtering out all positive aspects of a situation.

Polarized thinking

Things are black or white, good or bad; you must be perfect or a failure; there is no middle ground.

Overgeneralization

You come to a general conclusion based on one incident or piece of evidence; if something bad happens once, you expect it to happen again.

Mind reading

Without their saying so, you know what people are feeling and why they act the way they do; you are able to divine how people are feeling towards you.

Catastrophizing

You expect disaster; you notice or hear about a problem and start 'what ifs' – 'What if a tragedy strikes? What if it happens to me?'

Personalization

You think that everything people do or say is a reaction to you; you also compare yourself to others, to determine who is cleverer, better looking, and so on.

Control fallacies

If you feel externally controlled, you see yourself as helpless, a victim of fate; the fallacy of internal control has you responsible for the pain and happiness of everyone around you.

Fallacy of fairness

You feel resentful because you 'know' what is fair but other people do not agree with you.

Blaming

You hold other people responsible for your pain, or blame yourself for every problem or reversal.

Shoulds

You have a list of iron-clad rules about how you and other people should act; people who break the rules anger you and you feel guilty if you violate the rules.

Emotional reasoning

You believe that what you feel must be true – automatically; if you feel stupid and boring, then you must *be* stupid and boring.

Fallacy of change

You expect other people will change if you pressure or cajole them enough; you need to change people because your hopes for happiness seem to depend on them changing.

Global labelling

You generalize one or two qualities into a negative global judgement.

Being right

You must continually prove that your opinions and actions are correct; being wrong is unthinkable and you will go to any length to show your rightness.

Heaven's reward fallacy

You expect all your sacrifice and self-denial to pay off, as if someone was keeping score; you feel bitter when reward does not come.

The best tip-off that you are using distorted thinking is the presence of painful emotions. You feel nervous, depressed or chronically angry. You feel disgusted with yourself. You play certain worries over and over.

Ongoing conflicts with friends and family can also be a cue that you are using a distorted style. Notice what you say to yourself about the other person. Notice how you describe and justify your side of the conflict.

Your painful conclusions are based on fallacious rules. They result in misinterpretations, poor decision-making, lowered self-esteem, stressful emotions – and perhaps relapse.

The following 'matching' exercise set by Mathew McKay, Martha Davis and Patrick Fanning is to help you notice and identify distorted thinking. Match up each sentence with a distorted style of thinking, until all 15 distortions have been applied (answers at end of chapter).

Matching exercise (distorted thinking)

1 Ever since Lisa I've never trusted a good-looking woman.
2 Quite a few people here seem smarter than I am.
3 If you were more sexually open we'd have a happier marriage.
4 I worked and raised these kids and look what thanks I get.
5 You're either for me or against me.
6 I could have enjoyed the picnic but the chicken was burnt.

7 I feel depressed so life must be pointless.
8 You can't fight the system.
9 It's your fault we're always in the red each month.
10 He was a loser from the first day he showed up here.
11 It isn't fair that you can drink and I can't.
12 He's always smiling but I know he doesn't like me.
13 I don't care what you think. I'd do it exactly the same again.
14 We haven't seen each other for two days and I think the relationship is falling apart.
15 You should never ask people personal questions.

Again, eliminate your distortions by replacing them with positive, accurate attitudes, just as you did with your childhood messages.

DEALING WITH RECOVERY

Telling others

The way you tell your friends, family or employer that you are in recovery differs from person to person. If people are aware that you previously had a problem, it might be a good idea to let them know that you, too, have recognized it and are doing your best to recover from it.

It is not usually wise to go into any more detail about your addiction or your recovery. Indeed, healthy people do not usually want to know complex details, only that you are now 'on the mend'. I remember trying to tell a past employer that I had just started recovery. He stopped me almost mid-sentence and said 'All I care about is that you feel happier now'.

Another old friend, Laurence, with whom I had lost touch during the worst of my addictive behaviour and whom I also contacted in early recovery, simply said, 'But I always loved you; I was just concerned about you hurting yourself with your behaviour'. Hopefully, you will have similar unexpected loving experiences.

If people do want to know more, be honest with them. This applies particularly to your family – this is probably make-or-break time for your family relationships.

If you have children, you need to let them know that you have changed. No matter how young they are, they have been affected by your addictive behaviour. It might be an idea to wait until you have been a little while in recovery, by which time they will have noticed a change and can believe what you tell them. Also, if you had relapsed after telling them too soon, you would have raised false hopes and broken their trust. They would find it harder to believe you in future.

Before you talk to your children, read Appendix I which is about trying to prevent children from following in their parents' addictive footsteps. Apply its principles to your own children. Remember the false childhood messages and faulty thinking in this chapter, and try never to pass them on to your children. Give them the positive replacement messages instead. Mature together.

And remember that children do as their parents do. Your own healthy recovery is the best preparation for life you will both receive.

Getting help for your partner

Encourage your partner to attend Al-Anon, Alateen, Families Anonymous, Gam-Anon or other organizations which help the families of addictive people. If they do not like the meetings, they can at least pick up some literature to give them an understanding of what is happening and how they can be supported throughout your recovery.

Work

Choose your career carefully. It is important to most people to have a career rather than 'a job', but it is even more important to people in recovery. It has been said that up to 80 per cent of all grief comes from being in the wrong job. The difference between a career and a job is that the first offers hope and fulfilment, the second only money. You will lose that money if you relapse because of the unhappiness the job brings.

Having said that, many people in the first year or two of recovery take on simple work, usually volunteer work. This is ideal as it allows you to cope with all your new learning and life skills, practise managing your mood swings, and process the new emotions you are feeling. It allows you to practise bonding healthily with other people, perhaps for the first time. It means that you can concentrate on you and your needs and start to get a sense of self from what is within you, independent of the job you hold. This is particularly important for people with workaholic tendencies.

If you are in a high-stress job and cannot or do not wish to leave it, delegate or cut back on some of your responsibilities. Plan how much work you can achieve in office hours and stick to it. Because your mind is now clearer, you might find that some work is unnecessary, and that you take less time to achieve more of the necessary work.

Finally, choose the job sector you enter carefully. Working in a drinks-related industry, for example, is not a good idea; publicans and bar staff have the highest death rates from alcohol-related problems. Close behind are doctors, seafarers and lawyers. If you happen to be a qualified doctor or lawyer, there are special self-help groups for you (*see* Chapter 7).

Address any symptoms of workaholism. The following guidelines are recommended by Workaholics Anonymous:

- Prioritize – decide which are the most important things to do first, even if that means doing nothing; stay flexible, reorganizing priorities as needed.
- Substitute – do not add a new activity without eliminating from your schedule one which demands equivalent time and energy.
- Underschedule – allow more time than you think you need for a task or trip.
- Play – schedule times for play; do not make play into a work project.
- Concentrate – do one thing at a time.
- Pace yourself – work at a comfortable pace and rest *before* you get tired; do not get wound up in work so that you do not have to unwind.
- Relax – do not yield to pressure or try to pressure others; be alert to people and situations which trigger pressure in you; be aware of your actions, words, body sensations and feelings which tell you you are responding with pressure.
- Accept – accept the outcomes of your endeavours, whatever the results, whatever the timing; impatience, rushing and insisting on perfect results slow down our recovery.
- Balance your life – balance work involvement with efforts to develop healthy personal relationships, spiritual growth, creativity and playful attitudes.

Relationships

Don't rush into a relationship. Try to wait for a year – the further you are into your recovery, the healthier a partner you will choose. In early recovery, it is likely you will only repeat past experiences. Or that you will fall for a '13-Stepper', an oldtimer in self-help programmes who is adept at seducing vulnerable newcomers. S/he usually does not relapse on this – their victims often do.

Also, in early recovery it is easy to transfer your

addiction from whatever it has been to sexual activity or a specific person. You can find yourself spending time on them that you should be spending on your recovery. You can block out feelings you need to experience with a high from 'love' and lust. You have merely swapped one addiction for another.

Addiction freezes personality development so that, no matter what your chronological age, you are probably the emotional age of when you first starting using your addiction – usually this is the emotional age of an adolescent. For example, you might find yourself blushing and feeling awkward like you did when a teenager. You should be spending the first year of recovery maturing and advancing your interpersonal skills before you try to build a serious relationship.

The following questionnaire, from Wayne Kritsberg's *Family Intergration Systems*, can help you to determine whether you have become involved in a codependent, addictive, relapse-prone relationship.

Are You in a Codependent Relationship?

1 Do you place your partner's needs ahead of yours?
2 Have you ever hit or been hit by your partner?
3 Are you afraid to tell your partner when your feelings are hurt?
4 Does your partner tell you how to dress?
5 Do you smile when you are angry?
6 Do you have difficulty establishing personal boundaries and keeping them?
7 Is it difficult to express your true feelings to your partner?
8 Do you feel nervous and uncomfortable when alone?
9 Do you feel rejected when your partner is spending time with friends?
10 Do you feel shame when your partner makes a mistake?
11 Do you have sex when you do not want to?

12 Do you withhold sex to get even with your partner?
13 Do you think your partner's opinion is more important than your own?
14 Do you rely on your partner to make most of the decisions in the relationship?
15 Do you become very upset when your partner does not follow your plan?
16 Are you afraid to let your partner really know what you are feeling?
17 Do you keep silent to keep the peace?
18 Do you feel you give and give and get little or nothing in return?
19 Do you freeze up when in conflict with your partner?
20 Are you unhappy with your friendships?
21 Do you often find yourself saying 'It's not that bad'?
22 Do you feel you are 'stuck' in this relationship?
23 Must you control your emotions most of the time?
24 Do you lose control of your emotions during times of conflict?
25 Do you feel that your relationship would fall apart without your constant efforts?

A score of five or more 'yes' answers indicates that you might be or have been in a codependent relationship. The more 'yes' answers, the more dysfunctional the relationship.

If you are already in a relationship, it is usually advised not to make any decisions about it until a year has passed. There are exceptions, such as a woman in a violent relationship or with a partner tempting her to relapse. Women tend to relapse in response to a using male partner's encouragement more than men relapse in response to a female partner.

Getting into, or out of, a relationship can be a pivotal factor in most people's lives. Give it the importance it deserves by discussing it thoroughly with people you trust before taking any action.

Don't set yourself apart if you are gay. Some of the

fellowships in Chapter 7 have meetings specifically for gay people in recovery to meet each other and share common problems, experiences and solutions.

Coping with holiday times

Christmas and New Year are highly stressful events for anyone, as the high suicide rates at this time of year show. With recovering people, the stress is reflected in the high rates of relapse in late December and early January, and relapses in late January from complacency at having got through the first period.

Stress comes from having high expectations of Christmas and New Year, then having them disappointed. It comes from memories of shameful addictive behaviour during past Christmases and New Years. It comes from images all over the media of ideal happy families, something which addicts have usually either lost or never had in the first place. A gulf of emptiness opens.

Addicts can also feel that they must present a perfect image at this time, and this causes further strain.

One treatment centre says that its clients who are mothers feel overwhelming guilt. Many of them overcompensate by shoplifting expensive clothes and toys – which confuses the children.

So what preparations can you make to guard against relapse – and perhaps even have a good time?

1 Meet with some friends as early as November and discuss your fears. Share your fears at self-help meetings and with your therapist, if you have one.
2 Plan the event(s) well ahead. Account for as much as possible of your time with positive activities. Where do you want to spend Christmas? Do you want to spend it alone? With friends, family or other single members of your fellowship? Ask them, then enjoy planning together.

3 Keep things low key.
4 If necessary, use the emergency tactics in Chapter 4.
5 Some self-help groups hold meetings on the eve and day of Christmas and New Year. Go if one is available. Some groups also hold a New Year's Eve dance.
6 If going away, take recovery literature and tapes with you. Take soft drinks also, even if your addiction is not focused on alcohol. (There's no point in swapping poisons.) Serve your own drinks so no one can 'spike' them. If things get too much, go for a walk or to a room with privacy. Have a plan of escape ready in case things get worse.
7 If you must go to events of which you are fearful, ensure you have the means to get away quickly. Ask a friend to collect you at a certain hour. Have money for a telephone call to ring them sooner if necessary. Have the money for a taxi. Have a good excuse prepared. If you trust the host or a fellow guest, let them know that you must put your recovery first.
8 Stock up with lots of exotic soft drinks, so there is no excuse to go to an off-licence or public bar. Garnish them so they look special.

By surviving one Christmas and New Year, you learn that you can enjoy yourself without your addiction. You have set up a new 'building block' for future years. And I guarantee that the following year will be easier, because you will have good memories and experiences to draw on.

Other holidays away from home can be made easier if you find out in advance where self-help meetings are held, so you can express any fears and spend time with 'locals' in recovery. This is a huge advantage which members of self-help groups have that the general public does not: a way to meet local people quickly, with friendship and lots in common.

The following US-based agencies specialize in organizing trips for alcoholics in recovery:

- Sober Vacations 001–818–878 0008
  (email: www.sobervacation.com)
- Celebrate Life Tours 001–860–688 1100
- Serenity Trips 001–800–615 4665.

LETTING YOUR BODY RECOVER

The following lists of 'cleansing' foods for your body in early recovery, a 'growth' diet to keep your system balanced and natural health-care treatments, were devised by John Tindall, a London-based Chinese-medicine specialist in substance abuse, HIV and Aids.

Cleansing food

1 Fresh fruit and vegetables – cleansing
2 Wholegrains, eggs, fish, rather than meat and dairy products which burden the liver and kidneys
3 No greasy and fried foods which harm liver, skin and circulation
4 No sugar or refined flour products as they leach vitamins and minerals
5 Plenty of water and herbal tea
6 No tea or coffee, which leach vitamins and minerals

Growth diet

1 Eat protein and carbohydrate at separate meals
2 Alkaline foods, such as fruit and vegetables, to form 80 per cent of diet
3 No fluid with meals
4 Water to form 75 per cent of meal eg salads, lettuce, cucumber
5 Chew well

6 No emotional 'pigging out'. Eat only when hungry
7 Eat regularly

Natural health-care treatments

Acupuncture

Especially for acute withdrawal symptoms and chronic problems post-detoxification.

Shiatsu

Body work to release blockages and invigorate energy and for blood circulation.

Reflexology

Foot massage especially useful for insomnia, headaches, withdrawal pains and digestive disorders.

Hydrotherapy

Hot and cold baths for leg and back pains and to reduce acidosis (an abnormal increase in the acidity of the blood and extracellular fluids).

Essential oils

Very good for relaxation and muscle aches and pains. The most commonly used are lavender, ylang ylang and rosemary – use four drops of each in your bath.

Herbal teas

To cleanse and restore the internal chemistry of the body. For a special detox tea, use: camomile 1 part, scullcap 1, peppermint 1, catmint 1, yarrow 1, elder 1, vervain 1. Dose: 1 teaspoon of mixture in boiling water three times daily. To aid sleep use a tea made of camomile 1 part, motherwort 1, scullcap 1, passiflora 1, damiana 1, red clover 1, hop 0.25, lime flowers 1. Dose: 1 teaspoon of mixture in one cup of boiling water twice in the evening.

Moxibustion

For cold, weak, tired symptoms in chronic abusers. This is an ancient Chinese practice of warming points of the body to improve circulation, reduce pain and energize the internal systems.

Western exercise

To promote lymphatic and blood circulation and stimulate the release of endorphins, also fostering communication, team spirit discipline and acceptance of personal limitations. Examples: circuit training, rebounder, skipping, running, basket ball, volley ball.

Eastern exercise

Qi gong to integrate the mind, body and breathing in simple meditative movements or postures, to reach the highest level of self-realization. *Yoga* to release physical and mental tension and attain a raised consciousness.

Vitamins and minerals

To address the deficiency created by consistent drug abuse.
Vitamin C: 2g daily for adrenal and liver function, antibody formation, counter-acidosis and infections and capillary blockage.
Vitamin B complex: To repair nervous tissue, liver and skin.
Vitamin E: 400iu daily prevents destruction of vital fats, produces fatty hormones, improves liver function, reduces scars. (If you have high blood pressure, do not exceed 50iu daily.)
Vitamin A: 10,000iu daily improves eliminative function of the skin and mucous membranes, improves liver function, tones dry itchy skin.
Vitamin D: 1,000iu daily improves absorption of calcium and thus aids healing of nerves, bones and muscle.
Zinc: 30mg daily improves reaction to stress and helps treat inflammation and low fertility.
Iron: 10mg for anaemia (yellow dock).
Manganese: improves use of vitamin F, sterility, hyperactivity, bone and joint changes and pituitary weakness.
Calcium and Magnesium: For bone pains, nerves. Dolomite 300mg daily.

Relaxation

Try autogenics, relaxing exercise, meditation including transcendental meditation, biofeedback.

Finally, when for some reason none of the techniques in this or the previous chapters seem to be enough – *go to a self-help meeting or seek professional help*. The details are in the next chapters.

SOLUTIONS TO EXERCISES

Grief letter (*see* page 58)

You know that you have written this genuinely if it reads like a goodbye letter to a lover.

Distorted thinking (see pages 67–8)

1 Overgeneralization
2 Personalization
3 Fallacy of change
4 Heaven's reward fallacy
5 Polarized thinking
6 Filtering
7 Emotional reasoning
8 Control fallacies
9 Blaming
10 Global labelling
11 Fallacy of fairness
12 Mind reading
13 Being right
14 Catastrophizing
15 Shoulds.

CHAPTER 7

The Worldwide 12-Step Movement

A few years ago, the presenter on an American television chat show asked world-renowned diplomat Henry Kissinger what was the most valuable thing the US had given to the world.
'Alcoholics Anonymous,' came his reply.

Twelve-Step programmes, Alcoholics Anonymous (AA) and Narcotics Anonymous (NA) are becoming well-known organizations, and 'recovery' is a word rapidly coming into public usage. Characters in TV programmes and films drop the words casually. Sharon Gless, one of the two stars of the TV detective show *Cagney & Lacey*, had a storyline which showed her at AA meetings. Tim Robbins' character in Robert Altman's film *The Player* announced casually that he was dropping into an AA meeting not because he had an alcohol problem but to meet the film-industry contacts whom he knew would be there. In the 1997 film *Till There Was You*, Jeanne Tripplehorn and Dylan McDermott fell for each other after sharing an illicit cigarette outside a Smokers Anonymous meeting.

There are now 12-Step programmes for almost every addiction. But what are they and how can they help people to recover?

All 12-Step programmes are based on the earliest one, Alcoholics Anonymous, which was founded in 1935 by stockbroker Bill Wilson and surgeon Robert – 'Dr Bob' – Smith. Both had tried unsuccessfully for years to give up their addiction to alcohol – and succeeded only when they accidentally met and talked to each other about it.

Bill Wilson and Dr Bob decided to spread the message about what had worked for them, in the hope of helping other people with similar addiction problems. The infant society set down its experience in a book which reached the public four years later. At that time, the recoveries numbered only about 100.

The book was simply called *Alcoholics Anonymous*, often referred to as 'The Big Book', and from it the fellowship took its name. Its basic text remains unchanged through three editions, many reprints and millions of sales. It gives a history of AA, a clear understanding of alcoholism, and a way out of the addiction. Personal stories were added after the second edition, differing enough for any reader with a drinking problem to identify with at least one of them. The book spurred alcoholics to flock to AA in their tens of thousands. There are now millions of people in AA worldwide.

When AA's founders were 15 years sober, they collated the experience and knowledge gained from their own sobriety and from other members in the quickly growing fellowship. This was published as *Twelve Steps and Twelve Traditions*. It proposed to 'broaden and deepen the understanding of the 12 Steps as first written in the earlier work'. Its introduction explains that:

> AA's 12 Steps are a group of principles, spiritual in their nature, which, if practised as a way of life, can expel the obsession to drink and enable the sufferer to become happily and usefully whole . . . Though written mainly for members, it is thought by many of AA's friends that these pieces might arouse interest and find application outside AA itself . . . Many nonalcoholics report that as a result of the practice of AA's 12 Steps, they have been able to meet other difficulties of life . . . They see in them a way to a happy and effective living for many, alcoholic or not.

The 12 Steps now form the basis of self-help fellowships

for people with different addictions and for their families, friends, employers and others close to them. The following are the best known of the self-help organizations.

Al-Anon

For families and friends of problem drinkers.

Alateen

For the teenage children of alcoholics.

ACA, ACoA (Adult Children of Alcoholics)

For adult children of alcoholics.

Narcotics Anonymous

For people with a drug problem.

Families Anonymous

For families and friends of people with drug problems.

Gamblers Anonymous

For people with a gambling problem.

Gam-Anon

For the relatives of people with gambling problems.

Overeaters Anonymous

A slightly misleading name, as it is for overeaters, bulimics and anorexics.

Sex Addicts Anonymous

For people ruining their lives with compulsive sex.

Other fellowships, whose names are self-explanatory are: Codependants Anonymous, Cocaine Anonymous, Debtors Anonymous, Nicotine Anonymous, Pills Anonymous, Survivors of Incest Anonymous and Workaholics Anonymous.

There are also specialist 12-Step fellowships for addicts who are also doctors (eg The Doctors and Dentists Group), lawyers (eg The Lawyers Support Group) and nurses. These are separate from other groups because the members have many clients dependent on them whose interests need to be looked after while they themselves are being looked after. It is also to ensure confidentiality as these particular groups of people trying to recover risk being struck off the professional registers essential for their livelihood.

To write *Twelve Steps*, the authors daringly consulted leading figures in the then-embryonic field of psychotherapy, including Carl Jung. So thorough were the authors that anyone who today studies dynamic or integrative psychotherapy might be surprised to find that nothing in this 50-year-old book contradicts their learning. Certainly, there is nothing in it which modern teaching can contradict.

People who want to recover from their addictions can

get help from 12-Step meetings even before they apply the 12 Steps to their lives.

The first help, as the founders of AA discovered, comes from meeting people who have suffered or are suffering in a similar way. Most people who come to meetings believe that no one else is as bad as they are, no one else drinks/ drugs/gambles/binges/behaves as badly they do, no one else lies about it and hides it like they do. To find that other people have been or are in identical situations immediately lifts some of the shame which hampers recovery.

To discover that not only have other people acted as inappropriately as themselves, but that these other people miraculously *no longer do so* gives newcomers hope that they, too, can succeed like the solid, actual role models before their eyes. These people are not talking theory. They have lived the problem and have found the solution.

Going to meetings is also very practical in that it fills the time and the vacuum left by the addiction. When you are at a meeting, you cannot be in dangerous venues likely to lead to a relapse, or with users tempting you to do so.

If you say you are a newcomer, 'oldtimers' will give you their telephone numbers for you to ring when you fear you might relapse. Do ring them. They are only doing for you what someone else did for them when they were new. This is their way of returning the favour. And, hope-fully, when you are a few years into recovery, you will give your telephone number to newcomers.

Many people also go out for coffee and a chat after a meeting – 'the meeting after a meeting'. Merely by sitting and enjoying the chatter going on around you, you can learn that you can have fun and feel good about yourself without using an addiction.

The bestseller *The Road Less Travelled* by Dr M Scott Peck defines the difference between a child's love and an adult's love, which I see as a description of how 12-Step fellow-ships work.

Scott defines a child as 'being loved until s/he is able to

love' and an adult as 'loving until s/he is loved'.
Newcomers are like children in their emotions when they
come into a 12-Step fellowship. They are loved by oldtimers until they find their own capacity to love. Then,
with their new-found emotional maturity, they can love
newcomers who come after them. It sounds idealistic. But
it works extremely practically.

How fellowships work can also be explained by the
therapist Abraham Maslow's list of the five hierarchical
needs of all humans. These needs are called 'hierarchical'
because you cannot fulfil one need until the previous one
has been fulfilled.

Maslow names the first need as physiological: warmth,
food, water, shelter – and love. Experiments have shown
that baby rhesus monkeys die when deprived of their
mother's love. It is as basic as all the other physiological
needs.

Only when your physiological needs are secured can
you meet the second need: safety. Many addictive people
have never, as children or adults, gone past these two
stages. They have usually been deprived of love, through
abuse or the death of a parent. They have usually been
unsafe because of adults who shamed them, ignored their
needs, repressed their emotions, hit them or even sexually
assaulted them. The 12-Step fellowship is probably the first
time that they have felt loved and in the company of safe
people.

Because of this lack, addictive people are unlikely to
have reached the third hierarchy of need: a sense of
belonging and being loved. This is met, for many, again
only when they have found the fellowship of peers.

The fourth need is self-esteem and the fifth self-
realization. These will follow if you work through a good
programme of recovery.

What can you expect when you go to a 12-Step meeting?
First of all, you can make it easier on yourself by asking
someone to go with you. Simply telephone the relevant
'Anonymous' organization and ask for someone to

accompany you. This is a regular service they offer, called '12-Stepping', so do not feel that you are asking special favours. Otherwise, ask someone you trust.

When you enter a meeting, there is usually a 'greeter' who will introduce you to a few people and give you a 'starter pack' if you say that you are new to the fellowship. There is usually (free) tea and coffee, so that if you arrive early you can relax.

Meetings vary slightly in format and can last for an hour (if during lunchtime or rush hour) to an hour and a half (at other times). Usually, a 'secretary' starts by briefly explaining the format, stating that the fellowship is open to all who have a desire to stop their addiction, that there are 'no dues or fees' and asking for the 12 Steps to be read out. Then a 'speaker' is introduced.

The speaker usually talks for 20–30 minutes. S/he tells her/his own story, what happened to them during their addiction, how they came to see that they had a problem, how they tried to stop it, how they found the fellowship, and what they learned and are learning in the fellowship to help them maintain their recovery and a happier, more fulfilling way of life. Sometimes the speaker will talk of the problems in their life and how they are trying to solve them without their addiction.

The rest of the meeting allows other members of the fellowship to 'share' their own experiences. Sometimes they empathize with the speaker. Sometimes they have gone through similar problems and talk about the solution which worked for them. All this shared experience helps members to bond and to pick up positive feelings of hope and success.

Sometimes, 10 minutes of a meeting will be devoted to newcomers or people who find it hard to share. The more confident members will stay quiet so that they can do this.

Just before the end of the meeting, a 'pot' is passed round for voluntary contributions; put something in only if you can afford it. Then the 'serenity prayer' is said (see Step 3 later in this Chapter).

The size of the meetings can vary from half a dozen to over 150 people in popular central city areas. The members attending can be new and desperate for help or can have been in recovery for decades. Some AA meetings are attended by people who have not drunk for over 40 years! They are often asked why they still go, to which they reply, 'it's because I go that I'm still sober'.

Most people start going to meetings because they have to, but end up enjoying the companionship, help and support – a true fellowship.

You can also ask someone you trust in the fellowship to be your 'sponsor'. A sponsor is someone who agrees to help you with your recovery, particularly by guiding you through the 12 Steps. A sponsor is the person you can turn to first and most often when you are in difficulty.

Just one word of warning: there are some 'oldtimers', usually men in their 50s, who know that newcomers are very vulnerable and who have no scruples about borrowing money from them which will never be repaid or seducing them. It is hard to identify them because they usually speak well, but you will come to no harm provided you do not lend money to or go to bed with an 'oldtimer' in your first year. After that, you will be able to look after yourself.

Now, what are the 12 Steps and how can they help you to recover from your addiction?

THE 12 STEPS

1 We admitted we were powerless over [name of addiction] – that our lives had become unmanageable

The most important word of the 12 Steps is the first one: 'we'. The 12-Step fellowships work because people with similar histories meet to beat similar problems and to achieve recovery from addiction.

The first part of the sentence is the only part of all the

Steps to refer to the addiction, or to stopping the addiction. The other 11 Steps refer to a way of life which helps you to stay stopped.

The first part of the sentence is also important in that it is not until you, or the person close to you with an addiction problem, admits that there is a problem that action can be taken to find a solution.

The second part of the sentence looks at the unmanage-ability which the addiction has brought into addicts' lives: unmanageable marriage, other unmanageable relation-ships, unmanageable or precarious work situations, compromised value systems, unmanageable feelings and reactions, unmanageable behaviour, missed and late appointments, unmanageable finances ... the list goes on and on.

Looking at the damage which the addiction has caused provides a spur to staying out of the addiction.

2 Came to believe that a Power greater than ourselves could restore us to sanity

This sentence can also be interpreted as 'came [to the meet-ings] to believe' and 'came [eventually] to believe'.

A 'Power greater than ourselves' does not tie you down to any one religion or, indeed, any religion. It highlights that people used to make their addiction a power greater than themselves. Now you need a positive substitute, a substitute which protects your interests and health. You do not need to understand yet what that power is, just that there is something 'out there' which cares more for you than you do for yourself, respects you more than you do, and is looking after you.

For people who have problems with that, you can think of the people in your fellowship, with their experience and knowledge, as a power greater than yourself at this moment. Some people think of it as nature.

The 12-Step fellowships regard themselves as spiritual.

One definition of spirituality is that it occurs when your emotional, physical and mental sides all work in harmony. Another definition of the difference between religion and spirituality is that religion is for people who want to avoid hell whereas spirituality is for people who have been there. All addicts know what hell is like.

The last part of the sentence is 'could restore us to sanity'. One definition of insanity is 'doing the same thing over and over again hoping to get a different result' – also a good description of addictive behaviour. Insanity is trying to avoid unavoidable reality through addiction. Sanity is doing something different. Sanity is coming to a 12-Step meeting. Sanity is changing destructive behaviour into constructive behaviour.

3 Made a decision to turn our will and our lives over to the care of God *as we understood Him*

God, Power greater than ourselves, Higher Power . . . call it what you will, here we admit that our enormous willpower could not stop our addiction. Something else must come into the equation.

Step 3 says only that we made a decision, not that we *managed* to turn our will and our lives over to another power. All we need to do now is to make the decision.

This show of willingness, of letting go of willpower, is the first of the 'quality' steps, which bring relief, peace of mind and quality of life as we stop trying to control everything around us. The first two steps help us to stop our addiction. Now we learn how living a quality life means that we have avenues other than addiction to keep us fulfilled.

The chapter on Step 3 in AA's *Twelve Steps* ends with ' . . . it is really easy to begin the practice of Step 3. In all times of emotional disturbance or indecision, we can pause, ask for quiet, and in the stillness simply say *God grant me the serenity to accept the things I cannot change, courage to change the things I can, and wisdom to know the difference. Thy will, not mine, be done.'*

4 Made a searching and fearless moral inventory of ourselves

There are only three, simple rules to know about Step 4: that you must put it in writing; that the only way you can get it wrong is by deliberately lying or deliberately omitting something; and that you leave as little time as possible between Step 4 and Step 5.

A fourth rule is related to Step 5 but it is now that you must think about it: choose someone who can truly be trusted to go through Step 4 with you. This can be your sponsor – if you have not got one, find one for just this purpose – or even a therapist who understands the 12 Steps. Some people choose a priest.

Step 4 is a list of assets and liabilities in our nature, the good and the worse parts of our behaviour. Writing down the liabilities means that we can recognize them and change them. Sometimes, by the time we come to write down our liabilities, we realize that we started changing some of them as soon as we came into recovery. Others take longer to change. This is often the first time we start to see ourselves as we really are.

I mentioned in Chapter 2 that, when I came into recovery, I was asked what kind of person I was. Was I nasty or kind? Was I funloving? I could not answer. It was not until I started writing my Step 4 that I could see what assets and liabilities I had, and in what amounts. I started getting a picture of myself as a person rather than a work object.

When I wrote my first Step 4, I saw it as a test. My ideas about myself and my life had been validated so rarely that I did not know if my 'answers' were correct. A year later, I did a second Step 4 (this is not obligatory) and felt a wonderful sense of humility even as I was writing: I was not the best in the world at being bad, nor the best at being good. I was ordinary – and so were my actions. Even so, as I wrote out my assets I felt that I would be called a liar. Having my assets confirmed and validated was even rarer than having my reality validated.

Addictive people typically spend much time writing down their liabilities – but omit any mention of their assets. You must write down both to get a true picture. True humility is seeing yourself as you are, good and bad. Also, if you are overcome by all your defects you might feel too paralysed to move forward.

Take a break during your Step 4 if you feel tired or overcome by emotions. Telephone friends if anything you write makes you feel distressed. Telephone your sponsor. Start writing some assets. Finally, you can choose to do a bit of your Step 4, do a Step 5 on it, return to your Step 4, continue your Step 5, and so on.

'It is wise to *write* out our questions and answers. It will be an aid to clear thinking and honest appraisal,' says *Twelve Steps*. 'It will be the first *tangible* evidence of our complete willingness to move forward.'

I recommend Hazelden's excellent *Guide to Fourth Step Inventory* based on *Twelve Steps* for people who want to take this step.

5 Admitted to God, to ourselves, and to another human being the exact nature of our wrongs

'Scarcely any step is more necessary to long-time sobriety and peace of mind than this one,' states the *Twelve Steps*. In Step 5 we go through what we have written in our Step 4 with someone we trust. For most addicts, this is the first time in their lives they have been validated. After sharing their Step 4 with the listener, they often hear that that person has done the things they have done – often worse. They are not isolated by their past actions. Deeds which they previously thought were too shameful to put into words are put into perspective. Unuttered, they are a great amorphous fog; given a limited size on a piece of paper and compared to someone else's acts, they lose their power to instil fear and shame. They need no longer be drunk/ drugged/eaten/gambled/relapsed on.

And as you describe your assets, you will find that your Step 5 listener believes in your assets more than you do! They will have already seen them but will not have dismissed or minimized them as you probably have.

Shame and guilt paralyse people, not only addicts. Step 5 lifts these two debilitating emotions so that you can move forward.

The practice of admitting defects to another person is ancient – before counsellors there were priests. Psychiatrists and psychologists point out the deep need every human being has for practical insight and knowledge of themselves. It is no coincidence that addiction-treatment centres usually take their clients up to Step 5, then release them into the world to continue their development.

6 Were entirely ready to have God remove all these defects of character

In Steps 4 and 5, we identified our defects of character. Some of these have led to relapses in the past – and could do so again. Most have hurt us or others. Now we become willing to do something about them. We need not know what, just be willing. The key words 'entirely ready' underline the fact that we want to aim high.

The *Twelve Steps* sums up this step clearly.

Many will at once ask 'How can we accept the entire implication of Step 6? Why – that is perfection!' This sounds like a hard question, but practically speaking, it isn't. Only Step 1, where we made the 100 per cent admission we were powerless over [the addiction], can be practised with absolute perfection. The remaining 11 Steps state perfect ideals. They are goals toward which we look and the measuring sticks by which we estimate our progress. Seen in this light, Step 6 is still difficult,

but not at all impossible. The only urgent thing is that we
make a beginning, and keep trying.

For some people, attending therapy is Step 6 and Step 7
put into practice.

7 Humbly asked Him to remove our shortcomings

'Humbly' means with an understanding of both our assets
and liabilities. It means seeing ourselves as we truly are. It
does not mean humiliation, a word with which it is often
confused.

Now that we can see ourselves much more clearly after
Steps 4 and 5, and become willing in Step 6 to remove our
defects, we lay a foundation for the future. The *Twelve Steps*
states clearly:

> Without some degree of humility, no alcoholic can stay
> sober ... But when we have taken a square look at some of
> these defects, have discussed them with another, and have
> become willing to have them removed, our thinking about
> humility commences to have a wider meaning. By this time in
> all probability we have gained some measure of release from
> our more devastating handicaps. We enjoy moments in which
> there is something like real peace of mind. To those of us who
> have hitherto known only excitement, depression or anxiety –
> in other words, to all of us – this new-found peace is a priceless
> gift ... Where humility had formerly stood for a forced feeding
> on humble pie, it now begins to mean the nourishing
> ingredient which can give us serenity.

If the humility we used in Step 1 when we admitted we
were powerless over our addiction had a successful effect
then it can have a successful effect on our other, smaller
defects.

8 Made a list of all persons we had harmed, and became willing to make amends to them all

Twelve Steps promises that:

> Steps 8 and 9 are concerned with personal relations. First, we take a look backward and try to discover where we have been at fault; next we make a vigorous attempt to repair the damage we have done; and third, having thus cleaned away the debris of the past, we consider how, with our new-found knowledge of ourselves, we may develop the best possible relations with every human being we know.

Step 8 is writing a list of the people to whom you owe amends – bearing in mind that you probably owe more amends to yourself than to anyone else. To me, this is a grief list. List all your losses: not only deaths but also loss of relationships, friendships, jobs, money, and anything else which still disturbs you.

When you have finished, put an 'R' or an 'I' beside each entry. 'R' stands for retrievable, 'I' for irretrievable. You will be astonished to find how many are still retrievable. Don't act yet. Step 8 is only about making a list, not about acting.

You might have stolen from people or hurt them in other ways when you were in the throes of your addiction. Now you need to list them – you might already have them in your grief list under loss of relationship or job.

One good reason why Step 8 didn't come earlier is that you need a clear head to know who you might owe an amend to and who you don't. For example, I had so little esteem in early recovery that, if I bumped into a door, I would apologize to it. It was the same with people: I assumed I was in the wrong about everything. I wasn't. Once I wrote my list down, I found that I did not owe as many amends as I had expected.

'It is the beginning of the end of isolation,' says the *Twelve Steps* about Step 8.

9 Made direct amends to such people wherever possible, except when to do so would injure them or others

The first thing to remember about Step 9 is that it comes after Step 8 – not after Step 1. You need everything you have gained from the first eight Steps in order to do Step 9 correctly.

The second thing to remember is that staying away from your addiction is the best amend you can make to yourself and to everyone close to you. The longer you stay away from your addiction, the greater the amend is.

The third thing is not to make any amend until you have the self-esteem to face its consequences; an amend is not about humiliating yourself. The fourth thing is not to hope for a particular result from making the amend. There is no point, for example, returning stolen money to an employer in the hope of being re-employed. That is not what it is about. Step 9 is about restoring your conscience and peace of mind, so that you cannot relapse on your anxieties.

The fifth thing to remember is that an amend might not take the form you think. For example, stealing from a loved one cannot be atoned for by replacing the money. When you stole the money, you also stole their trust and peace of mind. These must be restored. You might have already gone a long way towards this by staying away from your addiction up to now, and reassuring them that you can continue to stay away from it and the behaviour which accompanied it.

The final part of the Step states 'except when to do so would injure them or others'. If your partner, for example, is now enjoying a new-found peace of mind because of your recovery, do not shatter it by revealing past affairs with other people. You will then owe an even greater amend for this hurtful so-called amend. It is also a good excuse to relapse.

Finally, you might want to make an amend to someone but feel that it is impossible because they are dead or untraceable. Here, you can make a 'proxy' amend, by making it to someone in as similar a situation as possible. One woman I know, for example, wanted to make an amend to the child she terminated. Her amend was to look after vulnerable mothers with young children, an amend to both her past situation and her unborn child. Other people write letters or poems to the dead, or carry out a specific wish they might have had.

10 Continued to take personal inventory and when we were wrong promptly admitted it

Step 10 is the only Step which gives a 'quick fix'. Say, for example, that you had a fight with someone close to you. Ask yourself: is it more important to be in the right or to retain the relationship? If you have been at fault, and can admit it to yourself, then a quick apology to the person with whom you have been arguing can save the relationship.

It can also save your recovery – resentment is a great prelude to a relapse.

One good idea in early recovery is to write down, just before you go to bed, all the pluses and minuses of the day – details of how you do this are on page 57. Some people make a more detailed inventory once a year or at longer intervals, to give themselves a spot-check and an overview of the progress they are making. This type of inventory has been called both a Step 10 and a Step 4.

11 Sought through prayer and meditation to improve our conscious contact with God *as we understood Him*, praying only for knowledge of His will for us and the power to carry that out

This sounds like the most 'airy-fairy' of all the steps, yet is the most practical. A half-hour's meditation at the start of the day can centre us for the rest of it. A walk or meditation in the park after an argument can give us the objectivity to put things in perspective and inspire us with a solution.

This is about letting go after all your earlier footwork, about trusting. 'When we refuse air, light or food, the body suffers,' the *Twelve Steps* explains. 'And when we turn away from meditation and prayer, we likewise deprive our minds, emotions and our intuitions of vitally needed support.'

For people who do not like the idea of praying, it recommends the following start by someone who, although he was not known to be an addict, did go through the emotional wringer that all addicts do.

> Lord, make me a channel of thy peace – that where there is hatred, I may bring love – that where there is wrong, I may bring the spirit of forgiveness – that where there is discord, I may bring harmony – that where there is error, I may bring truth – that where there is doubt, I may bring faith – that where there is despair, I may bring hope – that where there are shadows, I may bring light – that where there is sadness, I may bring joy. Lord, grant that I may seek rather to comfort than to be comforted – to understand, than to be understood – to love, than to be loved. For it is by self-forgetting that one finds. It is by forgiving that one is forgiven. It is by dying that one awakens to Eternal Life.

> St Francis of Assisi

'Perhaps one of the greatest rewards of meditation and prayer is the sense of *belonging* that comes to us. We no longer live in a completely hostile world,' writes the *Twelve Steps*. 'We are no longer lost and frightened and purposeless.'

**12 Having had a spiritual awakening as the result of
these steps, we tried to carry this message to [people with
our addiction], and to practise these principles in all our
affairs**

The 'spiritual awakening' is the physical, emotional and
mental awareness which comes to everyone who lives out
a programme of recovery and stays away from their
addiction.

'Carrying the message' is also known as '12 Stepping'. It
is when people who are in recovery help suffering addicts
towards Step 1. It is adult love, as opposed to childish love,
defined earlier in this chapter.

More formally, some fellowships allocate 12-Step rotas
where members volunteer to be available to take a telephone call from an addict in need, to visit and talk to them,
or to take them to a meeting. This is why newcomers
should never feel afraid to ask for help: they are helping
other members to fulfil their 12th Step.

Newcomers who think that a 12th Step is beyond them,
can do it simply by coming to meetings. A successful
meeting depends on at least two members turning up.
Everyone at a meeting keeps everyone else coming. That
is carrying the message.

'To practise these principles in all our affairs' means that
we live the principles of this programme. The 12 Steps are
not a theory or an intellectual opinion. They are a way of
life which succeeds in keeping people away from their
damaging, deadly addictions.

As the *Twelve Steps* explains:

Our basic troubles are the same as everyone else's, but when
an honest effort is made 'to practise these principles in all our
affairs', well-grounded [addicts] seem to have the ability . . .
to take these troubles in their stride and turn them into demon-
strations of faith. We have seen [addicts] suffer lingering
and fatal illness with little complaint, and often in good
cheer. We have sometimes seen families broken apart by

misunderstanding, tensions or actual infidelity, who are reunited by the [12-Step] way of life.

The joy of good living is the theme of the 12th Step.[1]

---

[1] The Twelve Steps are reprinted with the permission of Alcoholics Anonymous. Permission to reprint the Twelve Steps does not mean that A.A. agrees with the views expressed herein. A.A. is a programme of recovery from alcoholism only – use of the Twelve Steps in connection with programs and activities which are patterned after A.A., but which address other problems, or in any other non-A.A. context, does not imply otherwise.

CHAPTER 8

Relapses and Professional Help

INTERVENTION

The people who usually recognize the need for professional help first are the people affected by an addict's behaviour. But any attempt to get the addict to recognize their problem – far less do something about it – is usually met not only with denial of a problem but also anger, even rage. What can you do?

You can, of course, attend meetings for the families and friends of addicts (*see* Chapter 7) to help you cope with your feelings on a daily basis. You can also try a professional 'intervention'.

This is a gathering of an addict's family, close friends – sometimes even employer – and possibly a professional 'facilitator', usually seated in a circle, who try to persuade an addict that s/he has a problem and should seek treatment. Each person in turn starts by stating how much the addict means to her/him – but adds how damaged they have been by a *specific* behaviour or event caused by the addict. Addicts will usually not believe one person when they do not want to. But they cannot deny the cohesive opinions of many people, said not in anger but from love and a desire to help.

About nine out of ten interventions succeed in getting the addict into recovery. Even interventions which do not persuade the addict to start recovery now plant important seeds for the future. They also give family members the feeling that at least they tried.

A successful intervention helps not only the addict but all others present, since they can finally tell the addict how they have been hurt by the disease, and air their feelings and frustrations with a non-judgemental group. Through coming to recognize the problem for what it is, they can take steps to help themselves.

Before setting up the intervention, ask everyone who will be there to write a list of specific events and behaviours which have caused them pain. The more hard facts you have, the more effective the intervention will be.

Older children and adolescents are usually very effective participants in an intervention. But do not bring in young children who will need to be cared for and may distract you from the job in hand. Do not invite people whom you suspect might have an addiction problem of their own, as they could sabotage your efforts. And do not invite people who trigger anger in the addict, which could also sabotage your efforts.

It is usually best to ask a professional to facilitate the meeting, as they have the impartiality and experience to keep tempers down, to keep to the subject and not allow distractions, to keep things in perspective, to crystallize vague sentences and thoughts, to extract relevant information and to input specialist knowledge.

Arrange a preliminary planning and education meeting with the professional, so that you are prepared as much as possible for the intervention.

COUNSELLING

The facilitator might agree to take the addict on for counselling, or might recommend another counsellor, counselling agency or treatment centre. Alternatively, you might like to read up on what is available by way of treatment centres first and choose for yourself. You can find comprehensive lists in the US magazine *Professional Counselor* and the UK magazine *Addiction Counselling World*.

There are often waiting lists, so it might be a good idea to telephone the centre before the intervention, explain what you are doing, and time the intervention for a date when it expects a vacancy. If the intervention is successful, you do not want to waste a unique opportunity through waiting.

As an addict, you might have already realized that you need professional help, having found yourself relapsing into your addictive behaviour despite your best intentions and despite trying to carry out the recommendations in this book. This is no failure. Sometimes there is something behind the addiction which only a professional is qualified to deal with.

Specialists

Relapse-prevention specialists can ask their clients to commit themselves to six months' work on their recovery – a small slice of the rest of their lives. They ask 'What can you do to make it harder to relapse? How about turning off your money tap? Credit cards?' The suggestions come from the client.

Clients look at their contacts with alcohol/drugs/ addictive behaviour in their lives. They trace through pre-school, school and work areas on their psychological map. They look at childhood and adult friendships and relate them to addictive use. Next comes a chart of their relapse sequences. Gerald Deutsch, a Cenaps-accredited[1] relapse-prevention specialist, says that 'This, in my experience, is a staggering encounter for clients'.

Each relapse episode is then surveyed in closer detail. Tracing the history of a relapse is vital. It is then we can

---

[1] Cenaps (Centre for Applied Science) is a body which awards the most recognised relapse-prevention qualification.

identify the warning signs or 'triggers' to relapse, be they external, internal or a combination. Now the client learns to manage those warning signs or triggers.

So the treatment runs its course: trigger identification, trigger management and recovery planning. The plan is evaluated from time to time by therapist and client. It takes in all aspects of your life: work, relationships, leisure activities, exercise, diet, health and fun – just as in Chapter 6 but with temporary supervision.

There is no need, of course, for numerous relapses before seeking help from a counsellor/therapist for yourself or someone close to you. How do you choose? You do not go, as you might expect, to an institution representing 'general' counsellors, some of which do not recognize the need for specialist addiction counselling. Instead, turn to a specialist organization such as the National Association for Alcoholism and Drug Abuse (Naadac) which has branches worldwide (*see* Useful Addresses section).

You can also look for accreditation by the American Academy of Psychiatrists in Alcoholism and Addictions.

Naadac counsellors and therapists are usually in recovery themselves or have a family member in recovery. So they have knowledge and experience of addiction and how to recover from it. They are also invaluable role models: nothing inspires addicts looking for help more than someone who is living proof that you can be addicted and recover.

Another reason for choosing someone from Naadac is that the addict cannot fool them with excuses. 'You cannot con a conner', as the saying goes.

The reason I do not advise a 'general' counsellor or therapist at this stage is that they can drink, take drugs or act out addiction-prone behaviours in their own lives – recreationally or otherwise, and do not know how to treat people who must abstain totally. They also cannot provide an abstinence-free role model.

A 'general' counsellor can be appropriate when you are established in recovery and need to deal with an issue in which they specialize. By then, you will have a solid background of addiction-recovery work and can afford to see a counsellor who will concentrate on something else. When I was almost six years into recovery, I started seeing such a counsellor because of the post-traumatic stress disorder being triggered by a *current* situation. This was outside the area of addiction counselling.

However, always look for an abstinence-based counsellor or therapist. Word-of-mouth is the best recommendation. And, if you have a choice, choose the counsellor or therapist who seems happiest with life, who has the emotions you want to have. If your counsellor can enjoy life without addiction, it bodes well for an enjoyable abstinent life for their clients.

Ask your therapist, too, if they support 12-Step programmes. If they do not, it cuts out a large support network for the addict which can sustain her/him both during and after therapy has finished.

Some therapists work in private practice by themselves, others in an agency with other therapists.

Rights and responsibilities

The Standing Conference on Drug Abuse in the UK has published a *Service User's Charter of Rights and Responsibilities*. Designed for drug users, it can apply to all addicts looking for professional help. It states that the service provider – the counsellor or agency – has an obligation to make your rights and responsibilities explicit to you, as follows.

A drug service user has the right to:

- Assessment of individual need, within a specified number of working days
- Access to specialist services, within a maximum waiting time (and the right of immediate access on release from prison)

- Full information about treatment options and informed involvement in making decisions concerning treatment
- An individual care plan and participation in the writing and reviewing of that care plan
- Respect for privacy, dignity and confidentiality, and an explanation of any exceptional circumstances in which information will be divulged to others
- Referral for a second opinion, in consultation with a doctor, when referred to a consultant
- The development of service-user agreements, specifying clearly the type of service to be delivered and the expected quality standards
- The development of advocacy
- An effective complaints system
- Information about self-help groups and drug-user advocacy groups.

A service-user's responsibilities to the service provider include:

- Observing 'house' rules and behavioural rules, defined by the drug service – for example, not using drugs on the premises, treating staff with dignity and respect, and observing equal opportunities and no-smoking policies
- Specific responsibilities within the framework of a care plan or treatment contract – for example, keeping appointment times and observing medication regimes.

To the list of rights could be added choice of counsellor gender, where appropriate. For example, it is usually better to see a counsellor who is not of the same gender as the person(s) who maltreated the addict in the past, as this hinders the task of rebuilding trust. And ethnic-minority clients might want a counsellor who is sensitive to cultural issues. It is particularly difficult to get professional help for drinking Muslims, for instance, as on top of the usual addict's shame, it is against their religion to partake of alcohol in the first place. This issue must be dealt with.

Group counselling

Agencies may offer group counselling. This can start immediately or after you have learned to trust and share through individual sessions with a counsellor. When you go to an agency or counsellor, they will assess your needs and decide which type of counselling will suit you best and which counsellor is most appropriate for you. Their assessment will include whether individual or group counselling is most appropriate.

Group therapy usually consists of up to 10 people, usually sitting in a circle so that you can all see each other, with one or two counsellors, sometimes called 'facilitators' – this is to emphasize the fact that they facilitate, not run, the group. In other words, they encourage the members to interact with each other, and direct the group only when necessary.

It is decided in advance whether your group is closed or open ended. In the former, there is a predetermined number of sessions, usually between 6 and 12. The same people start and finish the group together, and newcomers are not usually allowed to join. The meeting might also centre round a specific subject matter.

An open-ended group can go on for an indefinite amount of time, can encompass a wide range of subjects, and might allow people to join in and drop out, so that the profile of its members keeps changing.

Groups consist of people who have had similar addictive problems. No one is worse or better than anyone else: you are all peers. You are about to discover together that you have similar solutions to those problems.

One member could start a group session by sharing a particular problem, either in the past or present. The facilitator usually asks if they would like feedback from other members about it. If agreed, the other members share their experience of similar problems and/or emotions, empathizing with the first speaker. Others might have already found a solution and can share this.

Group therapy allows members to learn to bond with like-minded people. It helps them to form healthy friendships. It helps them to open up honestly in front of other people. It removes the paralysing shame of past actions, as members learn that others present have done similar things. It helps members to see themselves more clearly as others react to them. And it helps them to confront others gently and with love. In short, it is good practice for life outside the group.

RESIDENTIAL TREATMENT

Sometimes, an assessment might show that an addict needs to go into residential treatment rather than day treatment. Residential treatment is divided into two kinds: first-stage and second-stage care.

First-stage treatment

This can last from four to eight weeks, depending on funding, where you go and on the progress you make. Progress does not depend on intellectual strides: it is about accepting the damage caused by your addiction, and about getting in touch with your feelings.

First-stage units are usually mixed gender. Most work is done in group sessions, as already described. A mixture of psychotherapies is used, to give a holistic approach: getting your mind, body and emotions to work together. It is when clients get in touch with their feelings that they feel complete. The emptiness, the vacuum, which had to be filled by anything – even dangerous addictive substances – is no more.

First-stage units based – sometimes loosely, sometimes tightly – on the 'Minnesota Model' link their psychotherapeutic approaches to the first 5 of the 12 Steps described in Chapter 7, and ensure that residents attend 12-Step meetings during their stay. This is so that when residents leave they will feel comfortable in meetings and benefit from their support for as long as they like after leaving treatment. Surveys show that almost all ex-residents who attend 12-Step meetings after treatment stay out of their addiction.

First-stage units can also offer yoga, meditation or other methods of relaxation where residents can learn to breathe properly and become more aware of their body. They are usually located in the countryside where residents can go on walks in beautiful surroundings. This brings an element of spirituality into residents' consciousness.

Because of the intense internal work residents must do while in first-stage care, they are cocooned from the outside world so that it will not interfere. Here they truly learn the meaning of 'keeping it in the day' for they are not allowed to look any further.

Residents usually finish with a Step 5, which allows them to move forward with a basis of self-knowledge, including identification of relapse triggers.

Sometimes, residents in first-stage care discover issues which must be investigated further before they can stay away from their addiction. A mother can have so many demands made on her by her family, for example, that she needs to learn how to deal with them before she returns home. Someone else might fear that if they return to their live-in drugging partner they will relapse, and need time to come to informed decision and action about this. Someone else might have discovered childhood-abuse issues which leave them vulnerable to more abuse; they need time and protection while exploring these further.

Second-stage treatment

In any of these cases, second-stage treatment might be recommended. You do not need to make any decision about this until you are about to leave first-stage care.

Second-stage care is less intense than first-stage. There might be one group therapy session a day rather than three. There might even be only one session a week. There is at least one individual counselling session a week. Again, many units recommend that residents attend 12-Step meetings so that there will be continuing support when they leave.

This is where residents learn to grab hold of their lives again. From a safe distance, they prepare themselves and their home, work or other situations for their return. There is much emphasis on boundaries and how they should be used in their individual home and work situations. Life skills can be taught, including training for a career. Where first-stage care has given a blueprint for the future, second-stage lays the foundations.

Many addicts might fear that they cannot get appropriate treatment because they have lost their money through their addiction. You can, of course, pay privately for treatment. But nowadays most people are funded by their insurance companies, their employers or government health benefits – although these tend to have longer waiting times. Your assessor can advise you where to apply.

PREDICTORS OF SUCCESS

There are no guaranteed predictors of successful recovery through treatment. However, one first-stage treatment centre in the south of England, Broadreach House, commissioned an independent researcher to assess its files of over 2,000 clients to see which denominators were common to clients who successfully completed treatment. The results, which have been reflected in surveys in other centres, were as follows:

1 The most powerful predictor of whether a client will complete treatment is their family's involvement, no matter how little.

2 The higher the status of the client's most recent employment, the better the outcome.

3 Female clients are more likely to complete treatment (probably due to the fact that female counsellors tend to be more successful).

4 Alcoholics are more likely to complete treatment than users of other drugs (this might be due to their higher socio-economic status).

5 The more years the client has been addicted, the better the outcome.

6 The shorter the wait to get into treatment once decided, the more likely the client is to complete treatment.

7 Previous contact with a self-help group is helpful – a little exposure is better than a lot, but this is better than none.

The two appendices look at treatment for specialist groups: adolescents, people forced into treatment, and people with other mental disorders or with physical disabilities.

CONCLUSION

Changing the Future

If you have read this far – congratulations! It shows a great determination to succeed.

You have in your hands knowledge which, sadly, many generations before us did not. You cannot change past history but you can change the future – and not only your own. Your positive actions in recovery will affect everyone in your family who sees or knows about the difference. Your relationships will change for the better and be with people who are good for you. If you have children, you can give them a head start in life by handing down your new-found knowledge.

There are people in this world who have said openly that they would not have won their Oscars or Emmys without recovery and the support of their self-help fellowships. They have given positive messages to millions of people through their talent. There are others in recovery who teach, who are nurses and doctors, who help people through the legal system, who give employment, who bring up children, who reach into readers' lives through their writings . . . The list goes on.

People in recovery are a great and invaluable talent. The world is richer for having them. Welcome.

APPENDIX I

Special Cases – Children and Adolescents

A parent with a three-year old child asked me when she should start educating the child about drugs. 'Now,' I replied.

SHARON SEABORNE
Manager of the Schools Education Programme
Drug & Alcohol Foundation, London

Any parents who want to do their best to prevent their children from becoming addicted must make a conscious effort to learn about four things:

- How to communicate with their children
- How to let their children express their feelings
- Boundaries
- Addiction

By reading all the chapters so far in this book, you will have made great inroads into the last two of the above. You might also need some knowledge about the specific drugs with which your children's peer group are experimenting. Pamphlets are now available, usually free, from government health departments.

By learning to express your own feelings through the previous chapters, you will also have made great strides in allowing your children to express theirs.

So we come to communicating with your child, something which cannot start too early.

PREVENTION

Until recently, it had been thought that the Australian government led the way in drug- and alcohol-prevention programmes for children, as it pioneered information about these on the school curriculum. But, seemingly against all logic, surveys show that this accelerated drug experimentation in children. What we have learned is that *how* we communicate information is vital. For example, a recovering addict who visits schools to talk about their addiction and recovery has more credibility with school-children than a teacher who lectures them.

Teenagers and young children today are faced with major challenges which leave them vulnerable to addiction and which did not exist in their parents' schooldays: the wide availability of mood-altering substances, peer pressure to be 'accepted' by using these, peer pressure to be accepted by getting a girl/boyfriend as early as puberty, family separations and 'blended' families when both parents take new partners. As ever, there are also family conflicts, and addicted or dysfunctional parent(s), with all the damage these can do to their children.

There is, of course, a difference between children abusing drugs and alcohol – which they can grow out of – and having a tendency to become addicted to them. To reassure yourself about what action to take, turn to the checklist on page 123 of this appendix.

Parents need to prepare for their child's adolescence, to be aware that their child is about to form a more autonomous personality and bridge the gap between childhood and adulthood. The information in the pages up to 123 comes from the experience of Dr Kathy Hirsch, a clinical psychologist from New York who specializes in child, adolescent and family development.

Adolescents experience psychological changes as well as the obvious physical ones. One US survey showed that parents unprepared for this suffered a mental-health deterioration as a result. Preventative measures are needed.

As the children go through puberty and adolescence, self-esteem becomes pre-eminent in shaping their future lives. And self-esteem is shaped here by three factors: appearance, popularity and intelligence. People's body image is usually formed in adolescence and will stay with them through their lives. If they think they are fat, they will always see themselves as fat, no matter how slim they are (you can see the potential for anorexia here).

Popularity depends on their peer group. If they feel inadequate, they can act this out by, for example, playing the clown or using drugs and alcohol. If the acting-out gives them a more 'successful' image with their peer group, they will continue to do it.

If you think that your child is 'acting out', you need to identify and address the issues they are struggling with – such as feeling unintelligent at school – to understand and address the behaviour.

A child's peer group forms part of her/his identity. Children aged 12 to 13 years old are most susceptible to outside influences such as this. Find out why a particular peer group attracts your child, so that you can encourage or discourage them from its influence.

These children are learning new social skills and how to form relationships. Parents see it as losing power, that their children are abandoning the values they taught them. Do not panic. Peer-group influence falls away from its peak at 12 to 13 years old. Parental influence continues into adulthood. Children are not separating from their parents. They are becoming connected in a new way.

At this time, parents feel unable to communicate with their growing children – while teenagers feel the same way about their parents.

How do you like people to respond to you when you are upset? Adolescents need the same consideration. If you cannot express your feelings, you will feel awkward allowing your children to express theirs.

Communicating with your child

Seven parental modes which close off communication with their children rather than opening it up have been identified by Don Dinkmeyer and Gary McKay in *The Parents' Handbook*.

Commander-in-chief

Typical phrases include 'shape up', 'pull yourself together' and 'set a good example'. The emphasis is on self-control, not the child expressing what is going on.

Moralist

Typical words and phrases include 'should' and 'should not' and orders to the child to have 'proper' or 'good' feelings – ie feelings with which the adult is comfortable. This again dismisses the child's feelings and closes the conversation. If this happens how can you bring up more important issues – such as addiction – later?

Know-it-all

The parent lectures, appeals to reason, shows that they are superior to the child.

Judge

The parent finds the child 'guilty' without a trial; the parent is always right, the child is always wrong.

Critic

The parent ridicules, name-calls, uses sarcasm and jokes.

Psychologist

The parent tries to analyse the feelings away, rather than allowing them just to be.

Consoler

The parent excuses themselves from involvement by treating emotions lightly; s/he gives a pat on the back and says the 'worries will disappear' or 'there are other children a lot worse off than you'.

How can you expect your children suddenly to open up about drugs or other addictions when their experience has been that you have shut them off as above? As soon as you change your attitude, you have started your addiction-prevention work.

The following is a basis for communicating with your children.

Aim for mutual respect

Express yourself honestly without fear of rejection and allow your child to do the same. You might argue with what your child is saying, but you must acknowledge the feelings.

Listen

Listen with your eyes by maintaining eye contact. Concentrate. Use body language which says 'I am listening', such as leaning forward, facing the child.

Observe

Observe nonverbal forms of communication: facial expressions, body language, tone of voice, general appearance, responses to others, attitude, who sits next to whom.

Validate

Let them know that you have heard them. Reflect and clarify their feelings. Restate them so that your child feels accepted. For example, your child might come home one day complaining that 'My teacher is unfair; I'll never do well'. Your reply could be 'You feel angry and disappointed; you have given up'. You have now opened up the communication.

Feedback

You have listened to, clarified and validated with your own comments. Repeat this with your child's next response (this is called feedback).

Educate

Give basic information about addiction and codependency in a way your child can understand. Help them to realize that any family problems are not their fault; introduce them to healthy living skills, including identification and expression of feelings, problem-solving, self-care strategies, and exercises building self-worth.

Empower

Help children to identify safe people to whom they can turn for support and guidance. Help them to realize they are not alone.

Open versus closed responses

In a closed response, the child does not feel heard or understood. You might feel that you have responded but have cut the lines of communication – refer to the seven parental modes. An open response reflects the speaker's message and allows the communication to expand.

*Listen and reflect **before** reacting*

Let your children learn. Resist the impulse to impose your own solutions. As children become adolescents, they must still have support but guidance and feedback replace demands and directives.

Adolescence is a smoother ride for parents who can remain active and involved with their teenagers. Teenagers need an authoritative, not an authoritarian approach. They need to feel that they have contributed to the rules. So agree a 'family set of rules' in which children have some input but the parents make the ultimate decision. They are then far more likely to keep those rules.

This is where boundaries come in (*see* Chapter 5). Children need to learn that breaking rules has consequences. Alcohol and drugs come under this heading.

Discuss them along with other rules, not as a particular subject in themself.

Why are children attracted to drugs? Why do they experiment? Some responses from Dr Hirsch's clients are:

- To escape
- I feel invincible
- It's fun
- To be accepted by my friends
- It's hard to say no to my friends
- It feels good
- I feel like an adult
- It relaxes me.

The response from children who do not use drugs is 'fear of disappointing my parents'. The response to being asked the difference between them and their friends who do use is 'I talk to my parents'. Your open communication is vital in trying to prevent addiction.

SUMMARY OF ADDICTION-PREVENTION MEASURES

1 Start talking early, and keep talking.
2 Look for moments when your children are receptive, but do not wait for ever.
3 Listen to your children; reflect back to them and clarify what they say.
4 Build a 'community check' with other parents (for example, if your child tells you that 'everyone' is going to a certain party, check with other parents).
5 Teach your children how to express their feelings.
6 Do not threaten; it only lowers credibility.
7 Roleplay situations such as peers offering drugs, being drunk, and so on.
8 Respect your children's behaviour when they say 'no' and become independent.

9 Praise your children when they are right and doing well.
10 Give them positive labels; for example, refer to their 'mature' behaviour.
11 Develop common interests: go to community events, sporting events, plays and films with your children.
12 *Be a good role model* – children do as their parents do, not as their parents say!

WARNING SIGNS OF TEENAGE SUBSTANCE ABUSE

- Fall-off in school work
- Withdrawal from others
- Chronic fatigue/lethargy
- Loss of interest in hobbies/sports
- Change in relationship with parents
- Chronic lying about whereabouts
- Sudden disappearance of valuables and money in the home
- Mood changes with no discernible cause
- Abusive behaviour to self and others
- Outbursts of inexplicable hostility
- Chronic dry, irritating cough/sore throat
- Chronic conjunctivitis otherwise unexplained
- Rebellious behaviour
- Isolation
- Change in friends.

It might come as a surprise to learn that the period between 3 and 6pm is when adolescents are most likely to succumb to alcohol, drugs or sex. This is because they are likely to be unsupervised as school has finished but their parents are not yet back from work.

YOU HAVE FOUND DRUGS/ALCOHOL IN YOUR CHILD'S ROOM: WHAT DO YOU DO?

- Do not panic.
- Do not shout.
- Wait 24 hours before saying anything and work out carefully what you want to say.
- Speak to a trusted friend, get feedback, go elsewhere for help.
- Talk to your child.
- Gather information: who, what, when, where, why.
- Punishment is best in the form of restricting privileges, such as use of the telephone. Give your child the power to redeem her/himself by learning to earn those privileges back. Teach your child that there is a consequence to the behaviour.
- Seek professional help.

CHILDREN FROM HIGH-RISK FAMILIES

Children who come from families in which addiction already exists are particularly vulnerable to becoming addicted themselves. One professional who specializes in prevention/intervention for children in high-stress, high-risk families is Jerry Moe, children's programme director at the Sierra Tucson addiction-treatment centre in Arizona and vice president of the National Association for the Children of Alcoholics. He says:

> The first concept for children to learn is that addiction and codependency are a family disease; everyone in the family gets hurt by it. The other two key concepts are for the children to accept that family addiction and codependency are not their fault, and that they are themselves at high risk for addiction and codependency.

He instils the three key concepts into the children, and helps them to realize they are not alone, that many children live in families with addiction and codependency problems.

The first day of his programme is called 'not my fault', and is about family addiction and codependency. The second day is 'all my feelings are OK'. The third is 'taking care of me' which is about problem-solving and self-care. And the fourth is 'I am special' which is about developing self-worth.

'Above all, it is important to love these children,' he recommends.

He has produced a workbook which can be used by parents, teachers and therapists – *Discovery: Finding the Buried Treasure* – which has exercises you can do with children from as young as four years old right through their childhood.

ABUSE AND ADDICTION

Some parents condone teenage use of alcohol and even 'recreational' drugs. But mood-altering substances will delay their development. More importantly, there could be life-long consequences due to irresponsible behaviour while under the influence. Joy-riding while drinking, getting pregnant or a sexual disease including HIV, and death from Ecstasy are some which spring quickly to mind.

It can be hard to distinguish between abuse and addiction in teenagers, as they do not have enough substance-abuse history to make a definitive diagnosis. It can help to look for the following characteristics, identified by Tammy Bell who has been working with adolescents since 1981. A lecturer and consultant, she is director of relapse-prevention services for the Cenaps Corp and a member of the Adolescent Treatment Consortium.

- Evidence of tolerance and withdrawal symptoms (*see* Chapter 2)
- Mental preoccupation and craving; preoccupation

includes thoughts of procurement, planning, actual use, euphoric recall and recovering from the effects
- How strong is the desire to use?
- What is the teenager willing to go through to do it?
- What is s/he willing to give up to use?
- How has substance use affected his/her interest in other areas of life?
- Loss of control
- Unable to stop, despite the consequences
- Tries to change circumstance, not substance use
- Is there a genetic predisposition?

It is important to spot the difference as early as possible, so that addicts can receive the appropriate treatment.

Bell cites the paramount importance of peer groups. Adults, no matter how much they have in common with adolescents through their addiction, are no substitute for an age-appropriate peer group. So self-help meetings packed with adults and adult-oriented treatment are not attractive to adolescents.

To get round this, Bell recommends that you ask an AA/NA member to escort an adolescent to their first few meetings. Recruit a temporary sponsor to mentor them for four to six weeks. This temporary sponsor can attend meetings with the adolescent, have post-meeting discussions to help them understand confusing concepts, and help relate the concepts to the adolescent's peer group, school, parents and others.

TECHNIQUES FOR PEOPLE 'FORCED' INTO TREATMENT

To get round the aversion to adult-oriented treatment, Bell runs a six-session weekly outpatient 'pretreatment' or 'motivate-toward-recovery' programme. This can also be used for people ordered by a court of law to get treatment and others 'forced' into treatment. It has three overriding themes:

1 Connecting life consequences to drug/alcohol use
2 Giving up the belief that they can control their drug/alcohol use
3 Controlled abstinence.

For the first, a group of adolescents are encouraged to 'brainstorm' their current problems and list them on a flipchart; 10 to 14 is a good number. Until then, adolescents believe that their lives are normal and their life problems have nothing to do with their alcohol or drug use. They feel that 'hysterical' or 'overreacting' adults are forcing them into treatment. They have not had time to evaluate their substance use.

Bell does not mention mood-altering substances at this stage. Instead, all she asks is that the clients study the list and see if they can work out the cause of the problems.

In the second session, she takes the list of problems back up and gets a new flipchart sheet headed 'Causes'. It is impossible for chemicals not to come up over and over again – but suggested by the clients, not Bell. The homework is simply to work on how to solve the problems.

When connecting life problems, find out which are important to the clients – for example being kicked out of school might not be, but getting a girl/boyfriend back is!

Almost all the clients come back to the third lesson suggesting that they must 'cut down' their use. If the adolescent is a social user, this will work. If it doesn't work, you probably have an addict on your hands.

Adolescents – like many adults – need to try control before abstinence. We must respect that, but without encouraging use. They need to discover for themselves what they can and can't get away with so that they are more highly motivated to do something about their habit. If you had pointed out to them that control doesn't work for addicts, they would have only counterreacted. This way, the first light goes on. There will be a reluctant, small admission. This is much more important than any lecture on addiction.

Bell warns people not to build in rewards for compliant clients or punish those who are truthful about relapsing. The latter are the better clients in that they are consciously experiencing the consequences of abusing chemicals.

At this stage, she and the client draw up together a plan of action 'now that we know you cannot control your drug'. They might suggest abstaining for a limited period, perhaps to prove something to a particular person such as a judge or parent. As they leave a session with her and before they try, Bell extracts a promise. 'I think you can do it. But just perhaps, maybe, you can't, will you promise to do something for me? In the unlikely event that you fail, will you try a treatment programme?' The clients promise because they are positive that they will not fail.

Now we move into the third and final phase: controlled abstinence. These clients do not make lifestyle changes. They continue going to raves where friends take drugs, for example. Adolescents have not yet learned to delay gratification and are ruled by impulses. They are also immersed in a drugs subculture. It will take time for them to learn why they must leave friends behind.

Family intervention is the final thing which Bell will use. She also recommends a 'vibrant, vital' role model aged between 16 and 18 years, with street credibility, to talk to the adolescents about their own recovery. When she first started working with adolescents and could not find someone in recovery who was their own age, a recovering 28-year-old biker gave a successful talk. 'Kids like something funky,' she explains.

While taking someone through pretreatment, three major goals are accomplished. There is a thorough assessment over the six to eight weeks of sessions. It allows the clients to work through pretreatment tasks. And it allows motivational counselling, so people are motivated towards recovery.

To repeat what was said earlier, one final reminder about trying to prevent addiction and about helping to maintain recovery: *children will do as you do, not as you say.* You must be a reliable role model.

APPENDIX II

Special Cases – Dual Diagnosis

Wine drunk with equal quantities of water puts away anxiety and terrors.

HIPPOCRATES

Hippocrates was right: wine and other drugs can mask mental unease. Some people recover from addiction – then find that they have diagnosable depression or schizophrenia which had been masked by their drinking or drugging. Others might had difficulty getting clean or sober, or constantly relapse, because they have a psychiatric disorder entwined with their chemical dependency. People who have both a chemical dependency and another psychiatric illness are described as having a 'dual disorder' or 'dual diagnosis'.

Like the word addiction, experts can disagree on the phrase. Some do not like to limit the number to 'dual'. Others say that any addiction can be included, but research to date has concentrated on chemical addiction.

Included under the heading of dual diagnosis are people whose even occasional use of alcohol or drugs causes problems serious enough to warrant treatment.

Studies indicate that drug or alcohol problems hamper the recovery of up to 75 per cent of psychiatric patients. So, if someone close to you has been having constant psychiatric problems, look at their alcohol/drug use. It might give you new hope for their recovery from the mental disorder.

For example, schizophrenics who drink can forget to take

their daily medication which keeps their lives manageable; address the drink problem and you will be addressing the problem of taking daily medication.

In 1990, the US National Institute of Mental Health published a survey of over 20,000 US adults. It found that 37 per cent of alcoholics had a mental disorder, and 53 per cent of drug addicts/dependents had at least one psychiatric disorder, as did 64 per cent of drug abusers in treatment.

The most common noticeable dual disorders are: bipolarity and schizophrenia (affecting more men than women) and depression (affecting more women than men), all of which are described in this appendix. The other most common dual disorders are personality and anxiety disorders.

The statistics are not as gloomy as they at first appear. For example, depressive symptoms can result from the effects of alcohol or drugs on the central nervous system. Most of these remit within a few weeks of abstinence.

Using or withdrawing from mood-altering chemicals can also result in mania, anxiety, panic, paranoia, delusions and hallucinations. For example, hallucinogen or stimulant users can become psychotic and appear schizophrenic. People who abuse tranquillizers can show agitation and anxiety symptoms when they cut back or stop using them. Deal with the addiction, and these states disappear.

Twelve-Step programmes emphasize the role of personality-change in the recovery process. Steps 4, 5, 6, 7, 10 and 12 in particular are about changing 'character defects', useful in dealing with personality disorders.

It is my experience that people who live a thorough programme of recovery from addiction, including counselling *with the right therapist*, deal with many mental disorders – without putting a psychiatric label on them – as they deal with their addictive way of life. Some of the issues which I know to have been effectively dealt with in counselling for addiction recovery include self-cutting/ self-mutilation, dependency disorders, antisocial disorders, chronic stress disorders including post-traumatic stress disorder and borderline personality disorders, and the effects of childhood abuse. This is why you must choose your counsellor carefully.

People with dual disorders are more likely to relapse than people without. But good therapy can mean a victory of dual recovery rather than dual relapse.

The suggestions for recovery throughout this book work not only for addiction but also help many dual disorders. Indeed, they are an excellent self-help tool if you have one of the above disorders, even without the addiction!

It must be stressed, however, that dual disorders need professional supervision. Some people might need psychiatric help and specialized medication.

Because dual disorders are a new area even for the professionals, read up on the subject if you suspect that you or someone close to you has a dual diagnosis. If you want even more information than this appendix, there is an excellent choice of inexpensive pamphlets and books on general and specific dual disorders from Hazelden worldwide and its European distributor Living Solutions (see Further Reading), including *Dual Disorders* by Dennis Daley, Howard Moss and Frances Campbell. In addition to this, the US magazine *Professional Counselor* is devoted to dual diagnosis, with each issue covering a different topic.

What is obvious as you read the symptoms of the mental disorders in this chapter is that they are very similar to people's traits when they are in active addiction. It is only when people stay out of their addiction that you can clearly see whether the symptoms really do belong to a mental disorder or whether they disappear with the addiction. In other words, if you or someone close to you exhibits the following symptoms, do not suspect a mental disorder unless they continue after a period of abstinence.

All the symptoms listed in this chapter are from the American Psychiatric Association's *DSM-IV*, the most widely accepted diagnostic manual worldwide. They apply only when the traits are not due to drugs/medication, a medical condition or another psychiatric condition. All traits must be inflexible and persistent, impair functioning or cause subjective distress.

MAJOR DEPRESSION AND DYSTHYMIA

'Major' is the most severe extreme of depression, and dysthymia the lightest. Both respond especially well to therapy correcting thinking and behaviour – including the suggestions in this book – as well as therapy exploring their nature. They also respond to medication.

About 14 per cent to 34 per cent of people with substance abuse disorders have current depressive illness; 35 per cent to 69 per cent of these might have it for life.

The following *DSM-IV* symptoms for major depression might occur during only one period in a lifetime or might be recurrent.

Symptoms for major depressive disorder

Two or more of the following occurring almost every day, when not due to a bereavement or other specific events:

1. Depressed mood most of the day
2. Decreased interest/pleasure in all, or almost all, activities most of the day
3. Significant weight loss when not dieting or weight gain (over 5 per cent of body weight in a month), or decrease or increase in appetite
4. Insomnia or hypersomnia
5. Restlessness or lethargy
6. Fatigue or loss of energy
7. Feelings of worthlessness or excessive or inappropriate guilt, not merely self-reproach
8. Diminished ability to think or concentrate, or indecisiveness

9 Recurrent thoughts of death, suicidal thoughts without a specific plan, suicide attempt, or a specific plan for committing suicide

10 There has never been a manic, mixed or hypomanic episode (see 'Bipolar disorders' below).

Dysthymia and major depression have similar symptoms, but they differ in onset, duration, persistence and severity. Major depressive episodes can be distinguished from someone's usual functioning but dysthymia has chronic, less severe symptoms which last for at least two years with less than two months' relief at a time.

For more information about the various types of depression read *Depression* by Sue Breton, another book in this series.

BIPOLAR DISORDER

Sometimes known as manic depression, this can involve 'manic' episodes, depressive episodes or both cyclically. Onset is usually before age 30 but can be after 50. In most cases, the first episode involves a swing into the manic state. About 60 per cent of people with a bipolar disorder have a chemical dependency, mainly alcohol.

It was explained to me that my 30 years of drinking had masked my manic depression. Psychiatrists told me that my adventurous and sometimes grandiose schemes – from organizing street festivals and concerts to risking death in the Sahara – were an indication of a manic inclination.

This was building when along came alcohol in considerable quantity. It was strong enough to suppress or distort the manic tendencies and at the same time increase the extent of any depressive periods.

I no longer drink alcohol. I follow a 12-Step programme. I also take non-addictive medication which is monitored with six-weekly blood tests. My life is manageable and I feel absolutely stabilized nowadays.

WYLTON, a dual-disorder recoverer

Wylton's story is similar to that of a few people I know in recovery with bipolar disorders. They have taken control of their lives to such an extent that, unless they speak of their condition, there is no way an onlooker could know they had a problem.

Symptoms for bipolar disorder, manic

1 There is a distinct period of abnormally and persistently elevated, expansive or irritable mood, lasting at least one week.
2 During the mood disturbance, three or more of the following are present:
    – inflated self-esteem or grandiosity
    – decreased need for sleep
    – more talkative than usual, or feeling pressured to talk
    – flight of ideas or feeling that thoughts are racing
    – distractibility (attention too easily drawn to unimportant or irrelevant external stimuli)
    – increase in goal-directed activity (socially, at work or school, or sexually) or psychomotor agitation
    – excessive involvement in pleasurable activities which could have painful consequences (eg shopping sprees, sexual indiscretions, foolish business investments).
    3 The mood disturbance is severe enough to cause marked impairment in occupational functioning or in usual social activities or relationships, or to necessitate hospitalization.

People can be treated in either an addiction-treatment or mental-health setting, but are more likely to be seen in the latter, and can be helped with self-help programmes – including the suggestions in this book – and therapy which addresses addiction. So a good programme of recovery can 'kill two birds with one stone'.

Sometimes these treatments are complemented with medication such as lithium, if the body lacks it.

SCHIZOPHRENIA

This is one of the most difficult dual diagnoses, but it is the degree to which a person has it which determines how successful treatment will be.

Symptoms for schizophrenia

1 Two or more of the following, each present for a significant part of a month (only one symptom required if the delusions are bizarre or the hallucinations consist of a voice keeping up a running commentary or more than one voice):
   – delusions
   – hallucinations
   – disorganized speech (derailment or incoherence)
   – grossly disorganized or catatonic (apathetic) behaviour
   – negative symptoms
2 Social/occupational performance falls markedly
3 The disturbance persists for at least six months.

It is particularly important to consult dual-diagnosis experts because treatments for schizophrenia and for addiction often oppose each other. For example, it is recommended that addicts express their feelings but that is not recommended for schizophrenics. Addicts must be confronted about their addiction but it is not recommended that schizophrenics are confronted about their illness.

Having said that, family involvement helps both the ill member and the family to get help for themselves. Success with schizophrenia comes in small steps but it can come.

And remember: when schizophrenics stay away from drink and drugs, they have more control over any medication which helps them to lead normal – even fulfilling – lives.

ANXIETY DISORDERS

These are the most common psychiatric problems in the general adult population. When you feel in danger, the normal reaction is 'fight or flight'. Your brain tells your body to feel fear from the danger – your adrenal glands secrete stress hormones, your heart thumps faster, blood is pumped to your muscles which tense for action, and sweat cools your body – and urges you to take one solution or the other. If you react like this to a danger that does not exist, or if you restrict your activities to avoid having such a response, an anxiety or phobic disorder exists.

Anxiety disorders include panic, phobic, obsessive-compulsive, post traumatic stress and generalized anxiety disorders.

Panic disorder

This is the most common anxiety disorder among clients seeking addiction treatment, and occurs twice as often in female drug abusers as male drug abusers. One panic disorder, agoraphobia or fear of open spaces, is the second most common dual disorder among alcoholic women. Parents, children and siblings of clients with anxiety problems tend to share that anxiety problem.

The *DSM-IV* defines a panic attack as a period of intense fear or discomfort in which four or more of the following symptoms develop abruptly and reach a peak in 10 minutes:

- pounding or accelerated heart rate
- sweating
- trembling

- sensations of shortness of breath or smothering
- feeling of choking
- chest pain/discomfort
- nausea/abdominal distress
- feeling dizzy/lightheaded/faint
- feelings of unreality/being detached from yourself
- fear of losing control/going crazy
- fear of dying
- numbness or tingling
- chills or hot flushes.

Sufferers can get relief through proper breathing and relaxation techniques, a healthy diet which eliminates stimulants such as caffeine and nicotine, exercise to reduce muscle tension, and techniques to correct thoughts and beliefs – in other words, many of the recommendations in this book. Temporary medication might be needed. One of the companion books in this series already mentioned, *Anxiety, Phobias & Panic Attacks*, can also help.

Phobic disorders

These are divided into 'social' and 'specific' phobias. The latter is an excessive or unreasonable persistent fear, triggered by the presence or anticipation of a specific object or situation. Examples are cats, spiders, flying, heights or receiving an injection. A social phobia is a persistent fear of social or performance situations in which you are exposed to unfamiliar people or possible scrutiny by others. You fear that you will act in a way which will be humiliating or embarrassing.

Both phobias can take the form of a panic attack. The avoidance of or distress at the situation interferes with your normal routine, work or social activities or relationships, and/or there is distress about having the phobia (incidentally, fear of eating in public is not usually due to a phobia but to anorexia or bulimia).

People with social phobias are best treated first in individual, then in group, therapy. When you resolve the social phobia first, you will feel more comfortable and do better in self-help programmes or other support groups.

Fear of social situations can be greatly reduced with training in good eye contact, posture, facial expression, voice quality and content and fluency of speech.

Obsessive-compulsive disorder (OCD)

Clinical anecdotes suggest that abuse of alcohol and minor tranquillizers is fairly common among people with obsessive-compulsive disorders.

Obsessions are persistent thoughts, impulses or images which are intrusive and cause anxiety. The most common are repeated thoughts about contamination (Howard Hughes is a famous example), repeated doubts (have I left the door unlocked?), a need to have things in a particular order, aggressive or horrific impulses (for example, to hurt your child or shout obscenities in church) and sexual imagery (recurrent pornography). These are unlikely to be related to a real-life problem.

Compulsions are other thoughts or actions which sufferers use to try to neutralize such thoughts and impulses. For example, if you are obsessed with contamination, you will compulsively vacuum-clean at midnight or scrub until the building stinks of ammonia. If you are obsessed with locking your front door, you try to neutralize the thoughts by compulsively checking to ensure that it is locked.

In some cases, you can perform rigid or stereotyped acts according to idiosyncratically elaborated rules without being able to indicate why you are doing them.

Obsessions or compulsions can displace useful and satisfying behaviour. Because they are distracting, they hamper cognitive tasks which need concentration, such as reading or computation. You might also avoid objects or situations which 'trigger' obsessions or compulsions. This avoidance can severely restrict general functioning. For example, a mother who was obsessed with shouting obscenities in church refused to attend her daughter's wedding.

People with OCD can benefit from behaviour and cognitive therapies, supported by medication. Reducing symptoms of this disorder reduces alcohol and drug intake, and vice versa.

Post-traumatic stress disorder (PTSD)

This is something I have found to be common among people who have experienced abuse in childhood, which is most addictive people. I am not detailing it in this book for the simple reason that the symptoms tend to be dealt with when you come into recovery, as you talk to your therapist about your childhood memories. These memories will surface only when you feel safe enough to allow them out, which is usually when you are comfortably into your recovery process. PTSD can be handled with your therapist, if you are free of mood-altering chemicals.

PERSONALITY DISORDERS

As with PTSD, I am not detailing **borderline personality disorder** for the identical reason that it tends to be automatically put in remission or dealt with as people talk to their therapists and follow a programme of recovery from addiction. This is the wonderful thing about a good recovery programme, as explained in this book: it helps in so many other areas of life.

Antisocial personality disorder (APD) is thought to be the most common personality disorder co-existing with addiction, and is found more among men than women. It is a pattern of disregard for, and violation of, the rights of others. People with APD can perform acts which are grounds for arrest, fight, be deceitful and lack remorse for the effects of their actions on others.

The good news is that many clients with APD can benefit from treatment, even if involuntary. The most effective therapy is to look at specific behaviours and ways of thinking rather than exploring the self.

Finally, there are people who have another type of 'dual' diagnosis, this time a physical one rather than psychiatric – people with physical disabilities.

NOT A SPECIAL CASE: PEOPLE WITH PHYSICAL DISABILITIES

Many people think that they must make allowances for people with physical disabilities who are addicted to drink, drugs or some other behaviour – but addiction is the most dangerous disability of them all. Indeed, the addiction might even have led to the physical disability, through accident or illness, in the first place.

People can mistakenly spend a great deal of time, energy and money treating symptoms rather than the addiction itself. This means little improvement for the disabled person and much stress for carers who can experience frustration, inadequacy, anger and physical and emotional exhaustion.

As Dennis Straw and Sharon Schaschl, two of the authors of *Substance Abuse & Physical Disability* state:

> Disability is commonly equated with illness, fostering the idea that disabled people are incapable of assuming responsibility for themselves, require repeated hospitalizations and must depend on mood-altering medication to function.

Straw and Schaschl are coordinator and consultant respectively at the Abbott Northwestern Hospital/Sister Kenny Institute in Minneapolis, USA, which in 1983 implemented an innovative chemical dependency/physical disability programme. They note:

> Family, friends and the medical community often feel that there is little value for disabled people in achieving a chemically-free lifestyle. It is assumed that, without chemicals, they could not cope with what is perceived as a miserable existence.

Some of their patients have received mood-altering medications since childhood and lived in protective environments which controlled their chemical use. When they left these environments and tried to integrate into an able-bodied society, increased chemical use became an equalizer. Addiction flourished.

Research on other patients, whose disabilities were the result of a later-onset trauma or illness, indicates that most were having problems related to mood-altering chemicals long before their disability.

The life problems experienced by people with disabilities – such as low self-esteem, poor hygiene, dependent lifestyle, lack of motivation, significant personality changes, memory deficits, depression, departure from personal values, isolation and unemployment – stem, as with all addicts, from the addiction and not from the physical disability. It cannot be made to be the excuse.

But change can be hard for carers, as allowing the addiction can ease their own uncomfortable feelings about the disability. Behaviours which are unacceptable in a non-disabled person might be permitted, ignored or excused in someone who has a disability. Addiction might be encouraged as a means of socializing and achieving equality with able-bodied friends or as 'one of my few pleasures'.

Carers might feel that they have no right to deny disabled people their choices, even if the choices are self-destructive. But carers often lose sight of their own choices as they are manipulated to give permission or assistance to the disabled person to carry out destructive behaviour.

As with all other addictions, mood-altering chemicals medicate feelings but feelings must be experienced and come to terms with. Disabled people can appear to express their feelings, but the chemicals keep them dissociated. Addiction treatment accelerates any emotional adjustment to the disability that is necessary.

So what medications are non-damaging? Medications are viewed in two categories, convenience and essential, according to Straw and Schaschl. Addictive, mood-altering muscle relaxants to control muscle tension (spasticity) and narcotics to manage chronic pain are convenience medications. Anti-convulsants to control seizures are essential medications.

Mood-altering, addictive medications are inappropriate for chronic conditions. Antidepressants are only appropriate when used with counselling and medical supervision.

Disabled people with chemical dependency must develop alternative methods of managing chronic pain, spasticity and stress. Relaxation, meditation, acupressure, biofeedback, self-hypnosis, diet, exercise, stretching, hot and cold packs, whirlpool and massage are effective replacement techniques. These methods can be developed independently or as part of a formal chronic-pain rehabilitation programme.

There seems to be about a three-month period after withdrawal of chemicals during which pain and spasticity intensify, as the nervous system adjusts to its unmedicated state and endorphin production is re-established.

Should someone be emotionally adjusted to his or her disability before entering treatment? Addiction stalls adjustment – addiction treatment accelerates it.

People with physical disabilities who have the courage to enter treatment might need help with writing materials/ tape recorders, buildings access and management of chronic pain and muscle tension. But they do not need special privileges.

Too often, disabled people have not been expected to take responsibility for themselves or their actions, and have learned to respond to the low expectations of others with self-pity, learned helplessness or manipulation. But acknowledging abilities allows disabled people to enjoy active and equal participation in recovery.

FURTHER READING

BOOKS

Alcoholics Anonymous, Alcoholics Anonymous World Service, New York, 1938

American Psychiatric Association, *Diagnostic and Statistical Manual of Mental Disorders, Fourth Edition (DSM-IV)*, American Psychiatric Association, Washington DC, 1994

Breton, Sue, *Depression*, Element Books, Shaftesbury, Dorset, 1996

Buckroyd, Julia, *Anorexia & Bulimia*, Element Books, Shaftesbury, Dorset, 1996

Daley, Dennis C, Moss, Howard B and Campbell, Frances, *Dual Disorders: Counseling Clients with Chemical Dependency and Mental Illness*, Hazelden Educational Materials, Center City, Minnesota 55012–0176 or Living Solutions, PO Box 616, Cork, Eire, 1987

Dinkmeyer, Don and McKay, Gary, *The Parents' Handbook: Systematic Training for Effective Parenting*, American Guidance Service, USA, 1989

Guide to Fourth Step Inventory, Hazelden, Center City, MN, 1973

Heinemann, Allen W (ed), *Substance Abuse & Physical Disability*, Haworth Press, New York, London, Norwood (Australia), 1993

Kritsberg, Wayne, *Family Integration Systems*, Health Communications, Deerfield Beach, FL, 1988

McKay, Mathew, Davis, Martha and Fanning, Patrick, *Thoughts & Feelings: The Art of Cognitive Stress Intervention*, New Harbinger Publications, Oakland, CA, 1981

Moe, Jerry, *Discovery: Finding the Buried Treasure*, Sierra Tucson Educational Materials, Arizona, 1993

Mooney, Al and Eisenberg, Arlene and Howard, *The Recovery Book*, Robinson, London, 1994

Peck, M Scott, *The Road Less Travelled*, Arrow Books, London, 1978

Sheehan, Elaine, *Anxiety, Phobias and Panic Attacks*, Element Books, Shaftesbury, Dorset, 1996

Twelve Steps and Twelve Traditions, Alcoholics Anonymous World Service, New York, 1952

Whitfield, Charles, MD, *Healing the Child Within*, Health Communications, Deerfield Beach, FL, 1989

—— *Co-Dependence: Healing the Human Condition*, Health Communications, Deerfield Beach, FL, 1991

—— *Boundaries and Relationships: Knowing, Protecting and Enjoying the Self*, Health Communications, Deerfield Beach, FL, 1993

MAGAZINES

Addiction Counselling World, Addiction Recovery Foundation, 122A Wilton Road, London SW1V 1JZ, UK

Professional Counselor, Health Communications, 3201 Southwest 15th Street, Deerfield Beach, FL 33442–8190, USA

USEFUL ADDRESSES

WORLDWIDE

Worldwide information on all the following addresses, and links to them, are available at *Addiction Counselling World's* website: http://easyweb.easynet.co.uk/~acw.

AUSTRALIA & NEW ZEALAND

Alcohol & drug addiction

Alchoholics Anonymous
Royal South Sydney Hospital
Joynton Avenue
2017 Zetland
Australia
Tel: 0061–2–663–1206

Al-Anon
GPO Box 1002-H
Melbourne
Victoria 3001
Australia
Tel: 0061–3–9629–8327

Naadac – National Association of Alcoholism and Drug Abuse
Counselors
Ross Colquhoun, president
15A 157 Crown Street

Central Chambers
Wollongong
New South Wales
Australia 2500

For information about treatment centres, workshops, publications

Queen Mary Centre Hospital
Private Bag 101
Hammer Springs 8273
New Zealand

CANADA & USA

Alcohol and drug addiction

Alcoholics Anonymous World Services (US and Canada)
475 Riverside Drive
New York
NY 10025
USA
Tel: 001–212–819–3400

Al-Anon Family Group HQ (US and Canada)
1600 Corporate Landing Parkway
Virginia Beach
VA 23454–5617
Tel: 001–757–563–1600

Cocaine Anonymous World Services
PO Box 2000
Los Angeles
California
CA 90094–8000
USA
Tel: 001–310–559–5833

Hazelden Foundation
PO Box 11
Center City
Minnesota 55012
USA

Naadac – National Association of Alcoholism and Drug Abuse
Counselors
1911 North Fort Myer Drive
Suite 900
Arlington
Virginia 22209
USA

For list of treatment centres and dual diagnosis information

Health Communications / Professional Counselor Magazine
3201 Southwest 15th Street
Deerfield Beach
Florida
FL 33442–8190
USA

UK & EIRE

Alcohol and drug addiction

Alcoholics Anonymous
PO Box 1
Stonebow House
Stonebow
York YO1 2NJ
UK
Tel: 01904–644026

Al-Anon
61 Great Dover Street
London SE1Y 4YF
UK
Tel: 0171–403–0888

Families Anonymous
Doddington & Rollo Community Association
Charlotte Despard Avenue
London SW11
UK
Tel: 0171–498–4680

Narcotics Anonymous
PO Box 1980
London N19 3LS
UK
Tel: 0171–251 4007

Hazelden Europe/Living Solutions
PO Box 616
Cork
Eire

Naadac – National Association of Alcoholism & Drug Abuse
Counsellors
375 Kennington Lane
London SE11 5QY
UK
Tel: 0171–582–6691

National Drugs Helpline (UK)
0800–776600

For list of self-help fellowships, treatment centres and other information

Addiction Recovery Foundation / *Addiction Counselling World*
122A Wilton Road
London
SW1V 1JZ

For list of treatment centres and addiction counsellors

EATA – European Association for the Treatment of Addiction
369–375 Kennington Lane
London SE11 5QY
Tel: 0171–582–6732

Shopaholism / compulsive spending

Patsy Hardy Centre
171 Beaver Road
Ashford
Kent TN23 7SG

Index